GRILLING, GRILLING & MORE GRILLING!

imagine!
Publishing

An Imagine Book
Published by Charlesbridge
85 Main Street, Watertown, MA 02472
617-926-0329
www.charlesbridge.com

Created by Penn Publishing Ltd.
1 Yehuda Halevi Street, Tel Aviv, Israel 65135
www.penn.co.il

Editor-in-Chief: Rachel Penn
Edited by Chaya Ben Shimon
Design and layout by Michal & Dekel
Photography by Danya Weiner
Assistant photography Sharon Novak
Food styling by Deanna Linder

Library of Congress Cataloging-in-Publication Data

Pilz, Dror.
 Grilling, grilling, and more grilling! / Dror Pilz ; photography by Danya
Weiner.
      p. cm.
 Includes bibliographical references and index.
 ISBN 978-1-936140-91-6 (alk. paper)
1. Barbecuing. I. Title.
 TX840.B3P546 2012
 641.7'6--dc23
                                             2012018518

2 4 6 8 10 9 7 5 3 1

For information about custom editions, special sales, premium and corporate
purchases, please contact Charlesbridge Publishing at specialsales@
charlesbridge.com

GRILLING, GRILLING & MORE GRILLING!

DROR PILZ

Photography by Danya Weiner

TABLE OF CONTENTS

MEAT

FISH AND SEAFOOD

SWEET ENDINGS

🔥

While traveling the globe in search of new culinary inspirations, I discovered that the most impressive and memorable food is not produced by expert chefs in the kitchens of five-star restaurants. Instead, it is prepared in the homes of food lovers who cook for the people they love—from the Midwest farmer's wife who churns her own butter to the Spanish olive grower who uses his grandfather's secret recipe for paella. In preparing fabulous food, professional expertise is far less important than the desire to serve a dish that makes a loved one smile.

Grilling, more than any other cooking medium, embodies the deep connection between food and the individuals who partake in it. Nothing draws friends and family together quite like the comfort of good company and the rich aroma of meat and vegetables cooked over an open flame.

My mother, to whose memory this book is dedicated, lived by the simple philosophy that food, family and friends should always mix, and she brought that wisdom to teaching me how to prepare unforgettable cookouts. Growing up in Romania, where harsh winters make food preservation a necessity, forced my mother to master the art of pickling and smoking. Even after leaving Romania, her love of traditional cooking techniques never dwindled, and her passion was passed down to me, along with her enthusiasm for turning simple ingredients into family-style gourmet.

Today, the great American melting pot has cultivated a culinary culture that celebrates the magic of fusion—the blending of East and West; of old and new. Similarly, the recipes in this book combine the time-tested grilling and preservation techniques I learned from my mother with the acumen of home chefs from around the world. This eclectic collection of grilling recipes, drawn from the beaches of the Mediterranean to the plains of South America to the rice paddies of the Far East, will help you show your guests that you care through the universal language of home-grilled food.

INTRODUCTION

The backyard cookout is doubtless the ultimate symbol of American camaraderie and prosperity. For generations, families have bonded, friends have reconnected, business deals have been struck, and milestones have been celebrated with the help of fine meats, a grill, and some basic know-how. Those of you who live in the northern and central parts of the country know only too well that the grilling days of summer are a precious few. That's why it's important to make the most of each and every gathering. What better way to create a lasting memory than by treating your friends and family to the sights, smells and tastes of expert grilling, using this book's easy-to-follow grilling tips and fail proof recipes.

🔥 Making the most of your summer cookouts requires a bit of "thinking outside of the box". Cookouts needn't be restricted to meats and cold salads. Vegetable dishes, baked pastries, pizzas and desserts can all be prepared on the grill. Think of your grill as an outdoor kitchen whose only limits are the boundaries of your imagination.

🔥 Serious meat lovers are sure to appreciate the smoking process. Traditionally used to preserve meat, today smoke cooking is purely for the sport griller's delight—it's a game of enriching aromas that adds dimension to meat's flavor, maximizing the savor.

🔥 Hosting a large number of guests can be accomplished easily with proper preparation. Making a specific list of the dishes you want to serve, as well as their ingredients, is an important factor in your cookout's success. I recommend arranging your food list according to cooking times. This will help you to time appetizers, entrées and desserts. Pay special attention to any recipes that call for marinating and prepare them in advance.

🔥 Check that you have the necessary ingredients on hand and, if possible, shop for ingredients the day before your event. Be sure you have taken into account the number of guests you expect to entertain, and purchase ingredients accordingly. Plan to serve at least 12 ounces of meat to each guest. Each diner is likely to consume 8 to 10 ounces of side dishes. And it's always good to make a little bit extra, so you can offer seconds.

🔥 Purchasing fresh vegetables and meats will make a substantial difference in the outcome of your dishes. Fresh meat is certainly preferable to frozen products, which tend to be tougher and less flavorful. To save time, wash vegetables before you begin to cook.

🔥 Using disposable plates and utensils for serving can significantly alleviate the stress of hosting by simplifying cleanup. I generally prefer to arrange the food on decorative serving plates and set out paper or plastic plates for the guests.

🔥 Having a well-stocked pantry is an essential part of your cookout's success. While no one has an unlimited amount of time to spend pickling vegetables and preparing marinades, you would be surprised at the amount of pantry basics you can accumulate if you prepare in bulk every time you grill and store the surplus in your freezer, refrigerator or pantry.

🔥 It's no secret that guests love to show up hungry! Instead of filling them up with heavy carbohydrates, such as bread with spinach dip and nacho chips with beans, give your guests a tantalizing preview of the grilled fare that awaits them by serving grilled sausage slices, mini kabobs or vegetable skewers. Slices of grilled chicken breast and steak served over a small bed of lettuce are also clever and easy starter options.

🔥 I recommend serving salads and breads alongside the main course rather than serving them before the meal. Intensify the flavor and texture of breads by brushing them with olive oil and grilling them until golden sear marks appear. Bread should remain soft on the inside while gaining a delightful crunch. Following this order of serving will not only make your cookout stand out from the rest, it will also help your guests feel lighter and ensure they still have enough room to enjoy the main course.

THE GRILL

For grill enthusiasts who regularly host cookouts, I recommend owning both gas and charcoal grills.

GAS GRILLS are designed for daily use. A distinct advantage of the gas grill is its ability to heat quickly, allowing you to prepare healthy meals, like grilled chicken and vegetables, within a matter of minutes.

Your grill should have cast-iron burners, enamel or cast-iron grate, a large grill plate and a grill cover. As for size, my philosophy is 'the bigger, the better'. Large grills give you the option of grilling several pieces of meat or different dishes simultaneously. The limited space offered by smaller grills may pose some timing problems if you are serving a large number of guests. Stores that carry patio and backyard supplies sell very reasonably priced medium-to large-size gas grills.

CHARCOAL GRILLS are best suited for slow grilling on weekends. Stainless steel grill grates are known for their durability and even cooking. Argentinean Asado-style, enamel-coated grill grates are a fantastic option, as their V-shaped grates catch juices and melted fat, which would otherwise create excess flame and smoke when they drip onto the coals.

Mastering temperature control on charcoal grills takes some practice. Many grills come with an adjustable firebox that allows you to control the distance of the coals from the food with an external crank. Putting distance between the food and the coals is the easiest way to control the heat level on a charcoal grill, and it is my preferred method. Alternatively, heat can be controlled by arranging coals on both sides of the food, or by arranging coals on one side and then cooking on the opposite side with the grill lid closed. (This is called indirect grilling.)

Whether cooking with a charcoal or gas grill, always remember that the grill is the star of the show. Have your guests' mouths watering before you've served a single sausage by positioning your grill within their line of sight, thereby treating them to a glimpse of the fare they're soon to enjoy.

THE GRILL STAND

In grilling, preparation is everything. It's important to ensure that your grill station is well stocked to avoid unnecessary trips to the kitchen that cost time and interrupt food preparation.
The following items should be readily available at your grill stand for every cookout:

- 2-3 towels
- Appropriate lighting for evening cookouts or shade for daytime grilling
- Barbecue mitts
- Basting brush
- Citronella candles to repel mosquitoes (for evenings) or fly traps (for daytime)
- Coarse salt and ground black pepper
- Cutting board
- Disposable wet wipes
- Knives
- Large coolers or buckets for cooling beverages in ice
- Long spoon or tongs for arranging coals (at least 14 inches long)
- Mixing bowls
- Refrigerator or cooler
- Skewers (Metal skewers are a long-lasting solution as they are reusable and do not burn. Bamboo skewers require soaking for at least 15 minutes before use so they don't burn on the grill.)
- Tongs
- Trash cans (at least 2)

EMBERS

The embers used in your grill can greatly influence the
flavor of your food. If using wood embers, seek out high-
quality apple wood, citrus wood or oak tree chips.
Ask a sales associate in your neighborhood grill store to
recommend professional grilling charcoals. High-grade
charcoal or woodchips can make the difference between an
average cookout and an unforgettable one!

LIGHTING THE GRILL

Light your embers with the help of lit newspapers or twigs.
Avoid using lighter fluid and self-starting charcoals, as
the chemicals in both can leave an unpleasant aftertaste in
your food. Lighting the charcoals with newspaper and twigs
may take a bit longer, but the outcome of natural tasting
food is certainly worth the wait.

Arrange briquettes in a pyramid-shaped mound atop
newspaper or twigs, and light the newspaper with a long
match. The fire from the newspaper and twigs will light
the charcoals. After lighting your charcoals, leave them
undisturbed for 30 minutes. Do not fan the charcoals.

The charcoals are ready when they are covered with
white ash and you can see that they are lit from within.
Use a pair of long-handled grilling tongs to scatter the
charcoals evenly across the bottom of the grill.

BEFORE GRILLING

• Heat the grill at least 10 minutes before placing the items you want to cook on the grate.
• Food placed on the grill should be at room temperature. Cold food should never be placed onto a hot grill.
• Be sure to take your meat and vegetables out of the refrigerator ½ hour to 1 hour before grilling to bring the food to room temperature and eliminate any extra moisture from the refrigerator.
• When cooking on a gas grill, it is best to heat the grill over a high flame and then lower the flame to the desired level before placing your food on the grate.
• Many charcoal grills are equipped with adjustable cooking grids, which will allow you to control the heat by changing the distance of the food from the coals.
• Similar to the gas grill, the cooking grid should first be warmed close to the coals, and then its height should be adjusted to obtain the desired level of heat.

GRILLING TIPS

RED MEAT — Sirloins and fillets are ready when they can be separated easily from the grill grate. You can test the doneness of the steak by touching it with the pads of your fingers.
• Rare — flesh is soft to the touch, giving
• Medium — flesh yields slightly to the touch or feels as though it is starting to firm
• Well done — flesh doesn't yield at all

Another good method of testing the doneness of red meat is with a meat thermometer:
• Rare — 125°F
• Medium — 140°F to 145°F
• Well done — 160°F

Avoid cutting steaks to determine their doneness, as this can cause the steaks to lose their moisture and flavor. Additional grilling option for red meat:

• Prime rib, sirloin and New York steaks can be grilled over a low flame or on a high-raised grill grid, turning frequently, until meat reaches desired level of doneness, or
• Seared on medium-raised grill grid for 1 hour. Cover the meat with aluminum foil and return to the grill grate to cook for an additional ½ hour.
• Ribs should be grilled on a medium-low raised grill grid for 2 to 3 minutes on each side. Slice and return to the grill to reach the desired doneness.
• Thin cuts of meat and hamburgers do not require any special grilling methods—simply place over a medium-low flame and cook until they are done.
• To roast meat, cook it on the grill with the grill lid down, or cover it with an aluminum dome plate cover.

CHICKEN — Unlike red meat, chicken must always be thoroughly cooked—no pink allowed! Chicken breasts should be grilled over a medium flame (when using a gas grill) or on a slightly raised grill grate (when using a charcoal grill). Whole and half chickens should be cooked slowly on a high-raised grill grid or over a low flame, turning occasionally. Another method for grilling whole or half chickens is to place the chickens on a metal cooking sheet on top of the grill grid. Grill over a high flame with the grill lid closed for ½ hour, then halve the chicken and grill directly on the grate until the chicken is lightly charred.

FISH — To prevent sticking, always brush the fish and the grill grate with oil before placing the fish on it. Grill fish over a very low flame or on a low positioned grill grate, once the charcoals are very weak.

SMOKE COOKING

Smoking, an ancient cooking technique once used to preserve meat and fish, is now the mark of the true journeyman sport griller. And while smoking lengthens the shelf life of any meat or fish, today's chefs smoke meats purely for the art of infusing a wide variety of flavors into prime cuts of meat. There are two types of smokes, hot and cold. Hot-smoked products are smoked in the same chamber as the burning wood, whereas cold-smoked products are held in an unheated chamber through which smoke is pumped (the smoke originating from an external firebox).

In both hot and cold smoking, meats are exposed to flavored smoke in a controlled environment for prolonged periods of time, allowing the smoke to disperse evenly throughout the meat and lock in the flavors it carries with it.

When executed properly, hot smoke cooking is as much a delight to the eyes and nose as it is to the tongue. During the smoking process, the color of the meat deepens and the meat absorbs the scent and flavor of the embers. Luckily, most gas and charcoal grills are equipped with a smoker. Specialty smokers are available at reasonable prices at most home improvement and department stores.

Smokers are generally cylindrical-shaped chambers containing a firebox to hold the wood chips, as well as one or two cooking racks placed above the firebox. As the smoke rises, it gently envelops the meat with the woody flavor. Many grillers insist that soaking wood chips in water is necessary for smoke cooking, but I have found that dry wood chips mixed with a bit of wet saw dust is just as effective. Moisture is, nevertheless, an important factor in the smoking process. I recommend placing a water pan above the embers in the smoker so that your meat will steam while it smokes, producing a tender and juicy result. The most essential element in smoke cooking is patience.

Think of it as a weekend sport; smoking is a marathon, not a race. Smoked meats need to be cooked at low temperatures (between 200°F and 225°F) for a minimum of 3 to 5 hours. Smoking time can vary, depending on the weather. For example, when smoking meat in a strong wind or at night, when the temperature is lower, you will need to smoke the meat for 4 or 5 hours, rather than 3 hours.

When smoking chickens, it is best to smoke a whole chicken rather than smoking small parts. Chicken should be smoked between 175°F and 250°F for 3 to 5 hours.

The process of smoking fish is slightly different, as the fish must first be soaked in brine and thoroughly dried before it can be placed in the smoker. Fish can be cold smoked between 110°F and 140°F for 20 minutes. I recommend perch, mackerel, trout and salmon for cold smoking. All other varieties of fish can be smoked in the same fashion as chicken or red meat.

WHAT TO SMOKE?

• Smoke cooking is an excellent method for transforming an average cut of meat into an exceptional dish. While prime fillets and expensive fish should be reserved for the grill grate, less pricey meats including chuck roasts, neck meat and plate meat come out juicy and tender when they're cooked slowly in the smoker.

• Virtually any kind of poultry can be smoked. However, birds with a gamier flavor, such as duck and goose, reach the height of their flavor potential when smoked. The best fish for smoke cooking are salmon, mackerel, perch and trout.

• Don't make the mistake of limiting your smoked selections to meat. The flavor of cheese and fruits can be enhanced through cold smoking as well.

CREATING THE FLAVOR

• Selecting the aromas and flavors to infuse into your meat is a matter of taste, so finding your perfect smoking recipe will take some practice. Luckily, options for experimentation are literally limitless.

• Smoked items are flavored by the wood chips they are smoked with. Each wood has a different essence to impart to your meat. For sweeter notes, try using wood from fruit trees, like apple or cherry wood. For heavier smoked flavors, try maple, hickory or mesquite wood. Combining two kinds of wood chips is a fine way to infuse even more flavors into your meat and vegetables, but be sure to pick two woods with comparable burning times and temperatures.

• To add more flavors, marinate meat and poultry before smoking. I love to add a variety of liquids to the water tray in the smoker, including wine, beer or soda; the evaporated liquid introduces another layer of flavor to the meat. Another method for amplifying aroma and flavor is to scatter dry spices over the burning embers in the final stages of smoking (in the last ½ hour).

MEASURING DONENESS

I use a simple skewer test to measure the doneness of the meat: insert a skewer into the meat and pay close attention to the liquid that is released when the meat is poked. If the liquid is clear, the meat is done. Reddish liquid is a sign the meat needs more time to cook. If no liquid is released from the meat, the meat is overcooked. Don't worry if your skewer test doesn't release any liquid—while overcooked meat is too dry to serve by itself, it will still be delicious in a sandwich. Allow smoked meats to rest for 10 minutes before serving.

GRILL SAFETY

When grilling, you are close to a live fire, so it is important to follow these guidelines:

🔥 When lighting a grill, keep the lid open.
🔥 Never leave a fire unattended.
🔥 Keep a fire extinguisher on hand.
🔥 Keep children away from a lit grill.
🔥 Take extra precautions when grilling on a windy day.

STORAGE

Smoked meats can be stored in the refrigerator for up to one week in plastic wrap, poked with holes. You may also place smoked meat in a vacuum pack and store it in the freezer for up to 2 months.

TIPS FOR HOT SMOKING

• Use good quality meat, poultry and fish. While it is true that smoke cooking is great for cheaper cuts of meat like chuck roast and plate meat, it is still important to select good quality meat.

• Smokers need to be properly cleaned and maintained. Ash and coals need to be removed after each use, and the chimney should be brushed clean. Do not clean the chimney with water or cleaning agents. It is best to cover your chimney when it's not in use.

• Avoid using pine wood embers in your smoker. While pine wood chips are often cheaper than hickory, apple and maple wood chips, the oils in coniferous tree wood produce a plastic-like aroma and flavor, and they burn too quickly to achieve good results.

• Avoid using lighter fluid to light your wood chips; the fluid can give meat an undesirable aftertaste.

• Evenly spread the embers in the smoke box. Do not place the meat in the smoker until all the embers are glowing. The wood should be grey and there should not be any smoke coming from the embers when you insert the meat into the smoker.

• Optimal hot smoking temperature is between 175°F and 250°F. I recommend using higher temperatures only for large cuts of meat, as heat can drastically reduce the moisture content.

• In order to prevent low-fat cuts of meat from drying out in the smoker, place a water tray over the embers so that the meat benefits from the steam. Refill the water tray when necessary.

• Opening your smoker releases heat; this will affect your overall cooking time. Give the meat an additional 5 to 10 minutes in the smoker for each time you open it.

TIPS FOR COLD SMOKING

• Unlike hot smoking, in which the product is placed on a grid over glowing embers, in the cold smoking process the embers are kept in an external firebox. The smoke is carried through a pipe to the chamber holding the product. This way, the product receives the smoke's flavor, but not the heat.

• The savory flavor and lush color fish will from this slow, delicate process will make the effort of cold smoking worthwhile. Cold smoking is used mainly for fish, but is also an excellent method for adding extra flavor to sausage and cheese.

• It is important to note that sausages and other meats should be grilled or baked after cold smoking, as cold smoking temperatures are not high enough to fully cook meat. For this reason, curing fish and meat is an important first step in cold smoking.

• When smoking, be sure to fill your firebox with a mixture of woodchips and moist wood shavings or sawdust.

• When smoking, the temperature in the firebox should be between 110°F and 140°F. An excellent method for maintaining a steady temperature in the firebox is to add 3 to 4 coals with the woodchips and sawdust—this will ensure that the fire is maintained for a longer period of time. Also, look for cool-burning woodchips, such as pecan.

• Because cold smoking requires a mild to cool climate, it is best to smoke fish during the fall and winter months.

THE PERFECT PANTRY

Grilling to perfection requires having a few key ingredients on hand, ready to use. The lists below will help you stock your kitchen with all you need to begin grilling your masterpieces.

FREEZER BASICS

- **Chicken stock, beef stock and vegetable stock** — Freeze stock in small portions and add to recipes as needed.

- **Chickpeas and beans** — Dry legumes must be soaked in water for 24 hours before cooking. It is important to rinse the beans and replace the water at least twice during the 24-hour period. After soaking the beans, transfer to a pot with water and bring to a boil. The beans should soften within 30 minutes. Beans can be stored in vacuum packs in the freezer for up to 3 months.

- **Crushed garlic** — Crush cloves from 3 heads of fresh garlic. Mix in a jar with ½ teaspoon of salt and 3 tablespoons of canola oil, and freeze. Garlic can be stored in vacuum packs in the freezer for up to 6 months.

- **Dough** — Stock your freezer with packaged tortillas, pre-prepared pizza dough (page 33), pita bread or any other kind of flatbread. Pita bread and flatbreads can generally be found in Mediterranean specialty stores and in fine supermarkets who sell organic goods or at organic stores. It is preferable to freeze your pita or flatbread on the same day that it was baked. If there is no freshly baked flatbread in your area, select the softest pre-packaged flatbread you can find in your local grocery.

- **Fried onions** — Julienne some onions and fry in canola oil. Drain the oil and store onions in sealed bags. Fried onions can be stored in vacuum packs in the freezer for up to 6 months.

- **Lemon juice** — Freeze juice from freshly squeezed, in-season lemons into an ice cube tray. Once frozen, transfer the juice cubes from the tray to a sealed freezer storage box.

- **Phyllo dough** — Ready-to-use packages of this leafy pastry dough can be found in most grocery stores.

- **Grilled eggplant** — Eggplant is a true chameleon. Its light flavor and texture are suitable for any combination of ingredients and seasoning, and it is equally delicious served alone. As if this vegetable's versatility were not magical enough, it also freezes beautifully, allowing you to have delicious grilled eggplant dishes well after the cookout season has closed. But no matter what fare you have in mind, it's important to remember that successful eggplant dishes begin with the right produce. Start by looking for fresh eggplant that is bright in color and light in weight. Grill eggplant over high heat, remove the skin and drain

eggplant of liquid. Grilled eggplant can be stored in vacuum packs in the freezer for up to 6 months.

REFRIGERATOR AND PANTRY BASICS

- **Feta or Bulgarian cheese, cubed**

- **Sheep or goat milk yogurt**

- **Greek yogurt cheese made from sheep milk or goat milk**

- **Tuna, sardines or anchovies**

- **Canned tomatoes**

- **Garlic confit** (page 18)

- **Fresh herbs** — Parsley, mint, cilantro and celery leaves. Rinse, dry well, wrap in a paper towel and store in a sealed plastic bag to maintain freshness.

- **Seasonal greens** — Arugula, garden cress, green onions, Swiss chard and lettuce should be staples in your refrigerator throughout the barbecue season.

- **Olive oil** — I recommend having 2 or 3 kinds of olive oil in your pantry. When it comes to grilling vegetables, Spanish olive oil is recommended, preferably one made from Cortina olives. Italian olive oil, made from Tuscan Leccino olives, is an incredible match for pastas. High-quality Mediterranean olive oil is ideal for seasoning vegetables and for preparing hummus and tahini sauce.

- **White wine vinegar**

- **Red wine vinegar**

ESSENTIAL SAUCES, SPICES & PASTES

GARLIC CONFIT

Makes

2

cups

Peeled cloves from 8 garlic bulbs
Olive oil (enough to cover cloves)

1. Preheat grill.
2. Place the garlic cloves in a clay or metal dish that is suitable for use on the grill. Immerse the cloves completely with olive oil. Cook on the grill over a low flame for 20 minutes, or until the oil comes to a gentle boil.
3. Remove from heat. Allow oil to cool, and place cloves and oil into sterilized jars.

Storage Instructions: Store confit in the pantry at room temperature for up to 1 month. It is important to keep the confit in a dry place as moisture can affect its flavor.

🔥 **A note from the chef:** Be sure to exercise caution when removing confit from the grill. Wear a barbecue mitt or another kind of protective gear to avoid heat and oil burns. To preserve the confit over time, it is important to always remove the garlic cloves with a clean spoon.

PICKLED LEMONS

Makes

1

medium jar

6 fresh lemons, cut into ¼-inch-thick slices
Salt

Salt the sliced lemons. Place in a sterilized jar. Seal the jar and let the lemons stand for 2 to 3 days. If the lemons appear dry, squeeze extra lemon juice into the jar and reseal. The lemons will become pickled within 4 days to 2 weeks.

Storage Instructions: Pickled lemons can be stored in the refrigerator for up to 6 months. To lengthen their shelf life, pour a layer of olive oil over the top.

🔥 **A note from the chef:** For the best result, I recommend using freshly picked lemons with thick rinds. If you don't have access to a lemon tree with ripe fruits, be sure to buy chemical-free lemons from any of the fine supermarkets who sell organic goods or at a farmer's market.

Pickled lemons are especially tasty when minced. The zesty tapenade is perfect for seasoning chicken, lamb and home-style tahini, and also makes an ideal substitute in any recipe that calls for fresh lemons.

🔥 Garlic Confit

THE COVERALL CLASSIC MARINADE

Makes

1

cup

½ cup olive oil
Coarse salt, to taste
Ground black pepper, to taste
2-3 cloves of garlic, crushed
¼ cup freshly squeezed lemon juice

1. Mix olive oil, salt, pepper, garlic and lemon juice in a bowl.
2. Taste and adjust seasoning with salt and pepper.

Make the perfect sauce for your dish by using the following variations:

For chicken breast – Combine oregano, dry mint and thyme with the olive oil, salt, pepper, garlic and lemon juice. Marinate the chicken breasts before grilling.

For salad – Add 2 tablespoons of vinegar, 1 teaspoon of sugar and 1 teaspoon of mustard to the olive oil, salt, pepper, garlic and lemon juice. Mix with lettuce and serve.

For fish – Add 1 egg yolk, 2 tablespoons of white wine vinegar and 1 teaspoon of mustard or horseradish to the olive oil, salt, pepper, garlic and lemon juice. Mix well and drizzle over fish immediately after it is removed from the grill.

For beef or chicken – Add freshly chopped herbs, such as cilantro, parsley or mint, to the olive oil, salt, pepper, garlic and lemon juice. Brush onto the fillets or cutlets before and after grilling.

<u>Storage instructions:</u> Marinade can be stored in sterilized jars in the refrigerator for up to 1 month.

🔥 **A note from the chef:** This basic sauce can be used as a marinade or a dressing, and is an excellent match for a variety of dishes including salads, poultry, fish and meat.

CHEF'S PEPPER MARINADE

Makes 2½ cups

¾ cup cayenne pepper
¾ cup sweet paprika
½ clove of garlic, crushed
Pinch of cumin
½ cup olive oil

Mix the cayenne pepper, paprika, garlic, cumin and olive oil together in a bowl.

Storage instructions: Marinade can be stored in a sterilized jar in the refrigerator for up to 1 month.

🔥 **A note from the chef:** This marinade provides a zesty kick to meat, fish and veggies. Brush on beef or poultry before grilling to bring out the marinade's heat.

PESTO

Makes 1 cup

3 cups fresh basil leaves, rinsed and dried
½ cup olive oil
4-5 garlic cloves
Coarse salt, to taste
Ground black pepper, to taste

1. Blend the basil, olive oil, garlic, salt and pepper in a food processor.
2. Taste and adjust seasoning with salt and pepper.

Storage instructions: Pesto can be stored in a sterilized jar in the refrigerator for up to 1 month.

OLIVE TAPENADE

Makes
1
cup

🔥 **A note from the chef:** Olives with pits tend to retain their flavor better than pitted olives. For a more robust tapenade, use fresh olives from your grocery's olive bar or look for unpitted olives in a jar, rather than pitted, canned olives. When using unpitted olives, be sure to use slightly more than 4 ounces to make up for the additional weight of the olive pits.

4 ounces pitted olives, preferably Tassos® or Kalamata
½ cup olive oil

Combine the olives and olive oil, and grind to a paste in a food processor. Transfer to sterile jars and store in the refrigerator.

Storage instructions: Tapenade can be stored in a sterilized jar in the refrigerator for up to 1 month.

01
BREAKFAST
& BRUNCH

EGGS A LA PLANCHA

This unique method for preparing eye-catching, sunrise-shaped eggs is a welcome departure from traditional frying and scrambling. Showcase in-season, fresh vegetables, cheeses and grilled meat with this unexpected egg delight. Prepare Eggs a la Plancha on the grill in a deep-dish skillet as a single serving, or make larger quantities in a cast-iron casserole. The skillet/casserole should have a cover.

SPINACH & FETA EGGS A LA PLANCHA

Makes

1

serving

A note from the chef: This recipe uses sumac, a North African spice derived from berries that is famous for its ruby red and purple hues. Sumac's lemony essence brings a touch of acidity to food without making it too tart.

1 pound spinach leaves, washed, soaked and chopped
½ cup olive oil
4 garlic cloves, peeled and halved
2 eggs
¼ teaspoon coarse salt
5 ounces feta cheese

For serving:
¼ teaspoon sumac (optional)

1. Preheat grill.
2. Boil water and a pinch of salt in a large pot. Add the spinach leaves and boil for 1 minute. Strain spinach from liquid and transfer the leaves to a bowl with ice. Chop leaves once cool.
3. Place a skillet on the grill grate, add olive oil and garlic, and sauté for 1 minute.
4. Add spinach, and break the eggs into the dish over the spinach. Season with salt and cover the dish for 1 minute.
5. Add feta cheese and cover the skillet. Cook for about 3 minutes until the egg whites are no longer transparent. Using a thick barbecue mitt, remove skillet from grill.
6. Arrange eggs, spinach and cheese on plate. Sprinkle with sumac and serve immediately.

SPICY CHORIZO SAUSAGE EGGS A LA PLANCHA

Makes

1

serving

🔥 **A note from the chef:** Seasoned with smoked hot paprika and garlic, chorizo sausages bring intensity to the eggs' mellow flavor. For gentler flavor, substitute bratwurst or chicken sausages for chorizo, and omit the cayenne pepper.

For the Ibérico Spice Purée:
1 tablespoon sweet paprika
1 teaspoon cayenne pepper
½ teaspoon salt
½ teaspoon black pepper
4 garlic cloves, crushed
½ cup olive oil

4 medium-sized tomatoes, quartered
Olive oil
2 links chorizo sausage
2 eggs

For serving:
2 tablespoons chopped cilantro or parsley

1. Preheat grill.
2. **Prepare Ibérico Spice Purée:** Blend the paprika, cayenne pepper, salt, black pepper, garlic and oil together using a food processor, or blend by hand with a mortar and pestle to form the Ibérico Spice Purée.
3. Brush the tomatoes with olive oil.
4. Grill the tomatoes and sausages until lightly charred. Using grilling tongs, remove first the tomatoes and then the sausages from the grill. The tomatoes should be removed from the grill well before the sausages.
5. Place a skillet on the grill grate. Add Ibérico Spice Purée and the grilled tomatoes.
6. Break the eggs into the skillet. Place the sausages over the eggs, cover, and cook for 3 minutes.
7. Using a thick barbecue mitt, remove skillet from grill. Remove lid. Transfer eggs, sausages, tomatoes and Ibérico Spice Purée to plate. Garnish with cilantro or parsley, and serve immediately.

MOZZARELLA, PESTO & GRILLED VEGETABLE SANDWICH

Makes

2

servings

4 tomatoes, sliced
8 small yellow bell peppers, sliced
Olive oil
Pesto (page 22)
4 slices bread
2 mozzarella balls, sliced

1. Preheat grill.
2. Brush tomatoes and bell peppers with olive oil, and grill until lightly charred.
3. Spread pesto over each slice of bread, covering the surface completely.
4. On one slice of bread, arrange grilled tomatoes and sliced peppers. Top with slices of a mozzarella ball. Close sandwich with a slice of bread.
5. Repeat Step 4 with remaining 2 slices of bread, mozzarella slices, grilled tomatoes and sliced peppers.
6. Toast both sandwiches, using a grill basket, until grill marks appear on the bread.
7. Using a thick barbecue mitt, remove basket from grill. Arrange toasted sandwiches on plates. Serve immediately.

A note from the chef: A grilled cheese sandwich fit for adult appetites! This sandwich is delicious with extra vegetables. Try it with sweet grilled zucchini or eggplant.

PIZZA

You don't need to be Italian to make delicious, authentic pizza with this simple dough recipe that is meant for cooking right on the grill. While it does take some time for the dough to rise, this pizza dough freezes beautifully, turning one Saturday afternoon of work into a freezer full of comfort food. After tasting your homemade grill-fired pizzas, your family will assure you that that making your own pizza dough was time well spent!

BASIC PIZZA DOUGH

Makes
6 to **8**
pizzas

🔥 **A note from the chef:** Selecting the right flour can make all the difference between average pizza dough and sensational dough. Use a finely ground, high-gluten flour of 12 percent protein for ideal results—a crust that is crunchy on the outside and chewy on the inside.

8 cups pizza flour
1 teaspoon salt
2 tablespoons active dry yeast
3 cups tepid water
1 teaspoon honey or molasses
½ cup olive oil

Olive oil for greasing
Toppings of choice

1. In a large mixing bowl, combine flour, salt and yeast. Knead with an electric mixer using a dough hook. Gradually add water.
2. Add the honey or molasses and olive oil. Knead dough for 4 minutes on low speed.
3. Raise the mixer's speed to high and continue kneading for 6 minutes.
4. Cover the bowl with a damp towel and allow the dough to rise until it has doubled in volume. This can take between 1 to 2 hours.
5. Remove the dough from the mixing bowl and knead by hand for 3 minutes.
6. Transfer the dough back to the mixing bowl, cover with the damp towel, and again allow the dough to rest until it has doubled in size.
7. Cut the dough into 6 to 8 pieces and shape dough into balls with your hands.

(continued on page 34)

(continued from page 33)

8. If you want to bake the dough immediately, place the balls of dough on a floured tray, cover with a damp towel, and allow dough to double in volume.
9. If you wish to freeze the dough for later use, wrap the balls of dough in plastic wrap or place each ball in a separate freezer bag and store in the freezer. The frozen balls of dough should be transferred to the refrigerator 2 days before you intend to bake them so that they can thaw thoroughly.
10. Preheat grill.
11. Grease a sheet of parchment paper with olive oil and press out a ball of dough using your hands. Brush olive oil over the top of the dough.
12. Flip the dough from the parchment paper onto the grill. Grill over a high flame. Within seconds, the dough will begin to bubble. Grill for 2 minutes and turn the dough with a spatula or tongs.
13. Using a pizza peel or a thick barbecue mitt, remove the pizza from the grill. Add toppings of your choice and if desired, cook the pizza on the grill with a closed lid for an additional 2-3 minutes.
14. Cut the pizza into wedges and serve immediately.

CLASSIC MARGHERITA PIZZA

Makes

1

pizza

🔥 **A note from the chef:** For pizza with a more complex smoked flavor, trade your charcoals for apple wood chips. Fresh or dry greens are an excellent way to garnish this classic recipe. Try topping your finished pizza with dry oregano and parsley, or with fresh basil leaves.

Basic Pizza Dough (page 33)
Olive oil
6 ripe tomatoes, peeled and grated
10 fresh mozzarella balls, sliced into medallions
Coarse salt, to taste
Ground black pepper, to taste

1. Preheat grill.
2. Grease a sheet of parchment paper with olive oil and press out the Basic Pizza Dough by hand. Brush the top of the dough with olive oil.
3. Flip the dough from the parchment paper onto a grill with a high flame. Within seconds, the dough will begin to bubble. Grill for 2 minutes and turn the dough with a spatula or tongs.
4. Spread grated tomatoes over the dough and arrange the mozzarella medallions. Taste and adjust seasoning with salt and pepper. Close the grill cover and bake for 2 minutes, or until the cheese bubbles.
5. Using a pizza peel or a thick barbecue mitt, remove the pizza from the grill. Cut the pizza into wedges and serve immediately.

PANCAKES ON THE GRILL

Nothing delights the brunch crowd like taking an old favorite and making it new, and pancakes are no exception. The following recipes help you reinvent the traditional pancake with exciting toppings that marry sweet and savory flavors for a combination your guests will not soon forget.

The foundation of these innovative recipes is a basic pancake, delicious on its own and strong enough to support toppings without losing the hallmark fluffiness of a pancake. I bet you will be making this basic pancake your go-to recipe, with or without the grill!

BASIC PANCAKES

Makes
20
medium-sized pancakes
(4-5 servings)

🔥 **A note from the chef:**
If you don't keep vanilla beans in the kitchen, feel free to substitute 1 teaspoon of vanilla extract.

¾ cup melted butter
4 eggs
2 cups milk
½ cup sugar
1 vanilla bean, cut lengthwise
4 teaspoons baking powder
1½ cups flour

Topping of choice

1. Preheat grill.
2. In a large mixing bowl, beat the butter, eggs, milk and sugar.
3. Scrape the vanilla bean with a knife and add seeds to the mixture. Add baking powder and flour, stirring lightly.
4. Heat a lightly buttered skillet. Pour a single scoop of batter into the skillet using a ladle. Allow the pancake to cook until its edges bubble, then flip and cook on the other side until pancake is golden on both sides. Remove pancakes from skillet. Place the pancakes in an aluminum foil pan and cover with aluminum foil. This keeps the pancakes warm while you cook another batch. Repeat until all batter has been used.
5. Using a thick barbecue mitt, remove skillet from grill.
6. Arrange stacks of pancakes on plates. Add topping of your choice. Serve immediately.

HAM & ASPARAGUS PANCAKES WITH DEMI-BÉARNAISE SAUCE

Makes 4 servings

🔥 **A note from the chef:** For extra smoked flavor, the ham may be cooked on the grill and then transferred to the skillet once light grill marks appear.

For the Demi-Béarnaise Sauce:
2 tablespoons olive oil
1 teaspoon Worcestershire sauce
1 tablespoon vinegar
1 tablespoon lemon juice
½ teaspoon sugar
Coarse salt, to taste
Ground black pepper, to taste

Olive oil
8 spears asparagus, trimmed
2-3 slices ham, chopped
4 eggs
Coarse salt, to taste
Ground black pepper, to taste
20 Basic Pancakes [page 36]

1   Preheat grill.
2. **Prepare the Demi-Béarnaise Sauce:** Beat the olive oil, Worcestershire sauce, vinegar, lemon juice, sugar, salt and pepper together in a bowl until a thick sauce forms. Taste and adjust seasoning with salt and pepper.
3. Brush olive oil on the asparagus spears and grill until lightly singed.
4. Warm a skillet on the grill and add ham. Cook until the color of the ham changes from pale pink to deep pink. Break eggs over the ham. Season with salt and pepper and cook for 3 minutes.
5. Arrange stacks of Basic Pancakes on plates.
6. Using a thick barbecue mitt, remove skillet from grill. Place the ham and eggs on top of the pancake stacks.
7. Top with grilled asparagus and finish by drizzling the Demi-Béarnaise sauce over the pancake stacks. Serve immediately.

SHRIMP & EGG PANCAKES

Makes

4

servings

1 tablespoon butter
3 medium-sized shrimp, peeled and deveined
2 eggs, beaten
Coarse salt, to taste
Ground black pepper, to taste
20 Basic Pancakes [page 36]

For serving:
2 tablespoons chives, chopped
2 tablespoons chili peppers, sliced

🔥 **A note from the chef:** Coupled with a fluffy pancake, this delicate mix of shrimp and eggs provides the perfect amount of protein to satisfy hungry brunchers. If you're not fond of shrimp, crab and lobster meat are palate-pleasing substitutes.

1. Preheat grill.
2. Melt butter in a pan over a hot grill. Add shrimp and sauté until the seafood turns a pink hue.
3. Add eggs to the pan and season with salt and pepper. Fry the eggs, sunny side up, stirring the shrimps occasionally.
4. Arrange stacks of Basic Pancakes on plates.
5. Using a thick barbecue mitt, remove pan from grill. Place egg and shrimp mixture on stacks of Basic Pancakes and garnish with chives and chili peppers. Serve immediately.

BRUSCHETTA

Bread is the base of every bruschetta. You don't need the finest bread in the bakery to make an excellent bruschetta, but you should give it some TLC before you add the toppings. Brush the bread with olive oil, season according to taste, and place on a hot grill for about one minute on each side. Always keep an eye on the bread while it's toasting—a few seconds too long on the grill can make the difference between perfectly toasted and inedible.

BACON & EGG BRUSCHETTA WITH SPICY MAYONNAISE

Makes

6

servings

6 slices bacon
6 slices smoked deli turkey
1 tablespoon mayonnaise
1 teaspoon Tabasco® Chipotle Sauce
Olive oil
6 eggs
6 slices bread, brushed with olive oil, grilled for 1 minute on each side

1. Preheat grill.
2. Using grilling tongs, place the bacon and turkey on the grill grate and allow meat to cook. Flip sides every 5 minutes for approximately 20 minutes.
3. Combine the mayonnaise and Tabasco® sauce in a bowl, and keep adding Tabasco® until the desired level of heat is attained.
4. Warm the olive oil on a very hot griddle, and then fry the eggs, sunny-side up.
5. Using a thick barbecue mitt, remove griddle from grill.
6. Arrange the bread on plates. Spread spicy mayonnaise over bread.
7. Place one slice of turkey and one slice of bacon on each slice of bread. Top with the fried egg and serve immediately.

🔥 **A note from the chef:** This soulful take on bruschetta breathes new life into the traditional 'bacon and eggs' breakfast. Select fresh artisan bread from your local baker and toast it lightly before topping it with the bacon and eggs.

BRUSCHETTA WITH BAKED BEANS & CHORIZO SAUSAGES

Makes

6

servings

🔥 **A note from the chef:** This recipe is the cowboy's answer to bruschetta—a true testimony to the culinary magic that happens when West meets East.

If you prefer sweeter beans, add a tablespoon of your favorite barbecue sauce to the mix.

1 teaspoon olive oil
1 teaspoon Tabasco® Chipotle Sauce
1 chorizo sausage
1 can baked beans in tomato sauce
6 slices bread, brushed with olive oil, grilled for 1 minute on each side
1 bunch cilantro, separated from the stems and washed thoroughly (optional)

1. Preheat grill.
2. Place a pan on the grill and warm the olive oil with the Tabasco® sauce.
3. In the meanwhile, grill the chorizo over moderately high heat, turning, until the sausages are browned all over and cooked throughout, for about 15 minutes. Once cooked, cut into ½-inch slices.
4. Add the beans to the pan, stir once, and cook for 3 minutes.
5. Arrange the bread on plates.
6. Using a thick barbecue mitt, remove pan from grill. Place 2 spoonfuls of the bean mixture on the bruschetta and top with 3 sausage slices. Sprinkle with fresh cilantro and serve immediately.

SAUTÉED CHERRY TOMATO & GARLIC BRUSCHETTA

Makes
6
servings

🔥 **A note from the chef:** Sometimes the simplest recipes are the most satisfying. To dress up this straightforward classic, place any grilled vegetable (see Grilled Vegetable Antipasti, page 53) on your bread before spooning on these flavorful cherry tomatoes.

2 teaspoons olive oil
30 cherry tomatoes
Coarse salt, to taste
Ground black pepper, to taste
6 slices bread, brushed with olive oil and
    grilled for 1 minute on each side

For serving:
10 Garlic Confit cloves (page 18)

1. Preheat barbecue grill.
2. In a skillet on the grill, warm olive oil and the cherry tomatoes.
3. Season with salt and pepper, and cook over low heat until juice runs out of the tomatoes.
4. Using a thick barbecue mitt, remove skillet from grill. Remove the tomatoes from the skillet and arrange them on top of the bread.
5. Garnish with Garlic Confit and serve.

MINTY GRILLED EGGPLANT BRUSCHETTA WITH GARLIC CONFIT

Makes

6

servings

1 medium-sized eggplant
6 Garlic Confit cloves (page 18)
1 cup mint leaves, washed and chopped
Coarse salt, to taste
Ground black pepper, to taste
6 slices bread, brushed with olive oil, grilled for 1 minute on each side

1. Preheat grill.
2. Use a fork to score the eggplant skin to prevent it from bursting while cooking.
3. Grill for approximately 20 minutes, turning several times during cooking, until eggplant is very tender when poked with a fork. Cooking time will vary depending on the size of the eggplant.
4. Using grilling tongs, remove eggplant from the grill and allow to rest until cool enough to handle.
5. Peel the skin from the eggplant, strain, and then chop.
6. In a bowl, mix the eggplant, Garlic Confit, mint, salt and pepper.
7. Spread 2 tablespoons of the eggplant mixture onto each slice of bread, and serve immediately.

🔥 **A note from the chef:** Eggplant, the "tofu" of all vegetables, adopts the flavor of spices and other ingredients within a dish. Because eggplant's delicate flavor is so malleable, you should take care to use wooden utensils to remove skin, chop, and mix the eggplant after cooking because metal utensils can leave a bitter taste.

Always grill eggplants on the highest possible flame and remove from the fire quickly. Eggplants are packed with water and should be strained for several minutes after grilling to remove excess liquids.

SWISS CHARD, CHICKPEA & FETA BRUSCHETTA

Makes

6

servings

🔥 **A note from the chef:** Swiss chard, also known as mustard greens or mangold, is a leafy vegetable that reveals a lemony flavor when exposed to heat. Because this green is seasonal, you may not be able to find it for the entire grilling season; however, kale, spinach and collard greens will make excellent substitutes.

4 leaves Swiss chard, washed and chopped
⅔ cup chickpeas, rinsed and strained
3 ounces sheep's milk feta cheese
1 tablespoon olive oil
1 teaspoon coarse salt
Juice from ½ fresh lemon
6 slices bread, brushed with olive oil, grilled for 1 minute on each side

1. In a mixing bowl, place Swiss chard, chickpeas, feta, olive oil and salt. Pour lemon juice onto the ingredients. Toss the salad until ingredients are evenly mixed.
2. Arrange salad on sourdough slices and serve.

02
SIDES
&
SALADS

EVERYBODY'S FAVORITE SMASHED POTATOES

Makes
6
servings

Salt
12 red potatoes, with peels
½ cup olive oil
1 tablespoon coarse salt
1 teaspoon ground black pepper
1 teaspoon brown sugar
1 tablespoon dry oregano

1. Preheat grill.
2. Add 2 shakes of salt to a pot of water. Boil potatoes until tender. Test the consistency of the potatoes by inserting a knife into the potato; when ready, the knife should slide easily into the potato. Strain and cool.
3. Hold each potato in the palm of your hand and squeeze lightly.
4. Season potatoes with olive oil, coarse salt, pepper, brown sugar and oregano. Place potatoes on grill, turning periodically until singe marks appear on all sides of the potatoes.
5. Using grilling tongs, remove potatoes from grill and transfer to dinner plates. Serve hot.

🔥 **A note from the chef:** Smashing potatoes produces a mashed potato like texture while locking in all the potatoes' flavor within its skin. If you find yourself without oregano in the kitchen, virtually any dry or fresh green herb, including parsley, rosemary, or marjoram can be used in its place. Surprise your guests by changing the herbs each time you serve the dish.

GRILLED VEGETABLE ANTIPASTI

Makes **10** to **12** servings

🔥 **A note from the chef:** Nothing intensifies the flavor of vegetables like grilling over an open flame. When a vegetable is cooked whole on the grill, it becomes a natural rotisserie—basting itself in its own juices from within the peel to maximize the flavor of the produce. Since there will be many vegetables on the grill, I recommend grilling smaller vegetables like mushrooms and cherry tomatoes on a skewer for faster turning and to prevent them from falling through the grates.

Some vegetables may become seared sooner than others. It is important to remove the vegetables once they have visible grill lines rather than waiting for all the vegetables to be fully cooked. Vegetables should be at room temperature when placed on the grill.

20 pieces okra
40 small peppers, various colors
40 cherry tomatoes
40 small onions or shallots
40 Champignon mushrooms
20 baby eggplants
10 beets
5 carrots
5 zucchini
5 spring onions
1 bunch asparagus (about 1 pound)
1 cup olive oil
1 head garlic, crushed
Coarse salt, to taste
Ground black pepper, to taste

1. Preheat grill.
2. Arrange the okra, peppers, tomatoes, onions, mushrooms, eggplant, beets, carrots and zucchini on metal or wood skewers. The spring onions and asparagus do not need to be skewered and can be placed directly on the grill.
3. In a mixing bowl, combine olive oil and crushed garlic.
4. Brush the garlic mixture onto the vegetables, and season with salt and pepper. Grill, turning periodically, until the vegetables are seared.
5. Using grilling tongs, remove from grill and transfer to dinner plates. Serve hot.

CAJUN CORN ON THE COB

Makes

6

servings

🔥 **A note from the chef:** Nobody does vegetables like the good ol' boys down south. Spicy, cheesy Cajun corn on the cob is served best alongside a juicy Surf and Turf Burger (page 79).

6 ears fresh corn, shucked and cleaned
½ cup melted butter
Coarse salt, to taste
Ground black pepper, to taste
½ cup Parmesan cheese, shredded

For serving:
1 teaspoon Tabasco® Sauce

1. Preheat grill.
2. Grill corn over a low flame, rotating frequently. This usually takes between 10 and 15 minutes, depending on the variety of corn.
3. Place corn on serving dish and pour the melted butter over it. Sprinkle with salt, pepper and Parmesan cheese, rotating the corn so that the entire surface gets covered.
4. Using grilling tongs, remove corn from grill and transfer to dinner plates.
5. Finish by dripping a few drops of Tabasco® sauce on each ear of corn. Serve hot.

GRILLED ARTICHOKES WITH FRESH YOGURT & MINT

Makes
4
servings

One 12-ounce jar oil-packed artichokes
½ cup goat's milk yogurt
1 clove garlic, crushed
1 tablespoon olive oil

For serving:
Olive oil
6 sprigs of mint, leaves only

1. Preheat grill.
2. Grill artichokes until lightly seared. Using grilling tongs, remove from grill and place on dinner plates.
3. In a bowl, mix the yogurt, crushed garlic and olive oil. Pour the mixture over the seared artichokes.
4. Drizzle with olive oil and scatter the fresh mint leaves over the artichokes. Serve hot.

A note from the chef: Artichoke's hearty, chewy texture makes it an excellent stand-in for meat. Grill extra artichokes to serve as a vegetarian entrée option with dinner, or add to green salads for extra volume.

ASIAN STYLE BOK CHOY

Makes
6
servings

🔥 **A note from the chef:** Bok choy, or Chinese cabbage, adds a dose of vitamin A to your spread. These meaty green vegetables are great on their own, or you can create a delicious cold salad by chopping grilled bok choy into a bed of egg noodles and mixing it with extra Tangy Asian sauce.

For the Tangy Asian Sauce:
½ cup sesame seeds
1 tablespoon brown sugar
2 garlic cloves, sliced
¾ inch fresh ginger root, chopped
3 tablespoons soy sauce
½ cup sesame seed oil

3 tablespoons canola oil or sunflower seed oil
6 bunches bok choy leaves

For serving:
Chili oil (optional)

1. Preheat grill.
2. **Prepare the Tangy Asian Sauce:** Toast the sesame seeds in a sauté pan until lightly browned. Transfer the toasted sesame seeds to a mixing bowl. Add the sugar, garlic, ginger, soy and sesame oil, and stir for 1 minute, lightly mashing the sesame seeds and garlic.
3. Heat a wok with oil on the grill. Add bok choy and sauté until slightly tender. Using a thick barbecue mitt, remove wok from heat.
4. Transfer bok choy to serving dishes and drizzle with Tangy Asian Sauce.
5. For an extra burst of flavor, lightly splash a few drops of chili oil over the prepared bok choy. Serve immediately.

GRILLED BEETS WITH COOL GREEK TZATZIKI SAUCE

Makes

6

servings

10 young beets with skins, washed and halved
½ cup olive oil
Coarse salt, to taste
Ground black pepper, to taste

For the Tzaziki Sauce:
1 cup Greek yogurt cheese
½ cup yogurt
¼ cup sour cream
½ cup olive oil
4 garlic cloves, crushed

For serving:
Olive oil

A note from the chef: Tzatziki, a tart, garlic-infused yogurt sauce, accentuates the sweetness of the beet for an incomparable harmony of flavors. Greek Tzatziki sauce is a winning complement for meats as well as fresh and grilled vegetables. Make extra Tzatziki Sauce to serve as a dip with your main course.

1. Preheat grill.
2. Oil the grill grate. Brush the beet halves with olive oil and grill lightly until tenderized. Using grilling tongs, remove beets from grill and transfer to dinner plates.
3. **Prepare the Tzatziki Sauce:** In a mixing bowl, combine the yogurt cheese, yogurt, sour cream, olive oil and garlic, and mix until smooth.
4. Brush the grilled beets with olive oil, sprinkle with salt and pepper to taste, and serve. Serve the Tzatziki Sauce in a dish alongside the beets.

THE KING'S CHICKEN CAESAR SALAD

Makes

6

servings

For the Baguette Croutons:
4 garlic cloves
8 slices baguette, sliced thick
¾ cup olive oil

4 Romaine lettuce hearts
1 large purple onion, thinly sliced
3-4 ounces Parmesan cheese, shaved

A note from the chef: The chicken marinade in this recipe is truly versatile. If you are already serving chicken at your meal, substitute the chicken for salmon or pork fillets. Vegetarians are sure to love this dish with marinated artichokes instead of chicken.

For the C¾hicken Marinade:
1 tablespoon olive oil
1 tablespoon lemon juice
1 teaspoon mustard
Coarse salt, to taste
Ground black pepper, to taste
Pinch of oregano

4 boneless chicken breasts, cleaned and sliced
   ½-inch thick

For the Caesar Dressing:
1 egg
½ cup olive oil
¼ cup vinegar
Juice from ½ lemon
1 teaspoon mustard
Coarse salt, to taste
Ground black pepper, to taste
½ teaspoon Worcestershire sauce

1. **Prepare the Chicken Marinade:** In a large bowl, mix the olive oil, lemon juice, mustard, salt, pepper and oregano. Add chicken breasts and marinate for 2 to 8 hours, depending on the desired concentration of flavor.
2. Preheat grill.
3. **Prepare the Caesar Dressing:** Begin by boiling a pot of water. Immerse the egg (in its shell) for 1 minute. Break the coddled egg into a mixing bowl, add the oil, vinegar, lemon juice, mustard, salt, pepper and Worcestershire sauce, and beat until thoroughly mixed.
4. Oil the grill grate. Transfer the chicken breasts from the Chicken Marinade to the grill, and sear on one side, for about 4 minutes. Turn and sear on the other side, until the juices run clear when the thickest part of a breast is pierced with a knife. Using grilling tongs, remove from grill and slice the chicken into 1-inch strips.
5. **Prepare the Baguette Croutons:** Dip both sides of the bread in olive oil and grill on each side, until bread is crispy on the outside and light grill marks appear on each side. Using grilling tongs, remove bread from grill. Rub ½ garlic clove onto each baguette slice and cut it into even-sized cubes, about ¾-inch to 1-inch wide.
6. Arrange the lettuce hearts on a flat, broad plate and place the chicken, croutons, onion and Parmesan shavings over the leaves. Drizzle with Caesar Dressing and toss lightly. Serve immediately.

MASHED POTATOES WITH GARLIC CONFIT

Makes
6
servings

🔥 **A note from the chef:** Potatoes take at least one hour to cook, so be sure to throw your potatoes on the grill well in advance of your meats, or boil them in advance.

12 potatoes, wrapped in aluminum foil and threaded onto a large metal skewer
1 cup Garlic Confit [page 18]
Coarse salt, to taste
Ground black pepper, to taste

1. Preheat grill.
2. **If using a charcoal grill:** Place the potatoes under the grill grate, on top of the charcoals. Allow potatoes to cook for 1 hour. Periodically turn the potatoes.
3. **If using a gas grill:** Spread a thin layer of cooking oil on a large sheet of aluminum foil. Use about 1 tablespoon for each potato. Wrap each potato individually in the aluminum foil. Place potatoes on grill over a medium fire, and cook for about 45 minutes, until they are tender when pierced with a knife. Periodically turn the potatoes.
4. Using grilling tongs, remove potatoes from grill and set aside to cool. Use a spoon to remove the flesh of the potato. Add Garlic Confit and salt and pepper to taste, and mix until a smooth purée is formed. Serve hot.

GRILLED CHERRY TOMATOES WITH THYME

Makes
4
servings

🔥 **A note from the chef:** When cooked on the grill, cherry tomatoes literally explode with flavor! They are great on their own as a side dish, or you can use them as a colorful addition to salads and pastas.

1 pound cherry tomatoes, with stems
Olive oil
Coarse salt, to taste
Ground black pepper, to taste
4 sprigs thyme

1. Preheat grill.
2. Place tomatoes in a skillet or grill-safe pan.
3. Drizzle generously with olive oil. Season to taste with salt, pepper and thyme.
4. Place the skillet on the grill over a low flame and cook until the tomatoes have softened and some of their juices have been drawn out. Using a thick barbecue mitt, remove skillet from grill. Transfer tomatoes to dinner plates. Serve hot.

Grilled Cherry Tomatoes with Thyme

GRILLED BUTTERNUT SQUASH

Makes
8
servings

🔥 **A note from the chef:** This vibrantly colored, sweet gourd makes an excellent substitute for starchy vegetables like potatoes and corn. In addition to being a wonderful accompaniment to meat, grilled butternut squash also complements eggs and pasta dishes.

3 butternut squashes, cut into ¾-inch slices
Olive oil

For serving:
Coarse salt, to taste
Ground black pepper, to taste

1. Preheat grill.
2. Brush the squash with olive oil.
3. Oil the grill grate. Place the squash slices on the grill over a low flame. After 2 minutes, turn the squash slices and grill for 1 additional minute.
4. Using grilling tongs, remove the squash slices from the flame and place in a serving dish. Sprinkle some salt and pepper onto the squash and serve.

STUFFED EGGPLANT ROLLS WITH RICOTTA & PESTO

Makes
6
servings

🔥 **A note from the chef:** This dish combines the refreshing zing of basil with the fruity undertone of pistachio for a flavor that is as unexpected as it is delicious. For variety, green zucchini makes an excellent substitute.

3 medium- or large-sized eggplants, sliced lengthwise about ⅓-inch wide
Olive oil
4 tablespoons Pesto (page 22)
16 ounces fresh Ricotta cheese
⅓ cup pistachio, chopped

For serving:
½ teaspoon coarse salt

1. Preheat grill.
2. Brush eggplant slices with olive oil. Grill slices on each side until light grill marks appear. Using grilling tongs, remove from heat and transfer to a baking dish.
3. Spread a layer of Pesto on each of the eggplant slices. Place a dollop of Ricotta in the center of each of the eggplant slices and spread cheese out evenly toward the edges of the eggplant, using more or less Ricotta according to your preference. Sprinkle pistachios evenly on eggplant slices. Roll each eggplant slice and close with a toothpick.
4. Sprinkle coarse salt over the top and serve.

ROMANIAN EGGPLANT SALAD

Makes
8
servings

3 medium-sized eggplants, grilled
4 red peppers
Olive oil
6 garlic cloves, crushed
1 teaspoon salt
½ cup vinegar
½ cup sunflower seed oil
½ teaspoon sugar

🔥 **A note from the chef:** Grilled eggplant can be prepared on a gas or charcoal grill. However, I recommend the latter, as the flavor of charcoal-grilled eggplant tends to be richer. Eggplant should be grilled as quickly as possible on the grate over an extremely high flame until its skin is charred. Be sure to thoroughly strain your eggplant before adding salad ingredients.

1. Preheat grill.
2. Use a fork to score the eggplant skin to prevent it from bursting while cooking.
3. Grill for approximately 20 minutes, turning several times during cooking, until eggplant is very tender when poked with a fork. Cooking time will vary, depending on the size of the eggplant.
4. Using grilling tongs, remove eggplant from the grill and allow it to stand until it's cool enough to handle.
5. Peel the skin from the eggplant and strain.
6. Brush the red peppers with olive oil and grill, until the skin is charred on all sides.
7. Using grilling tongs, remove the peppers from the grill and allow to rest until cool enough to handle.
8. Peel the skin from the peppers.
9. Chop the vegetables with a square wooden spatula and mix together in a bowl.
10. Add garlic, salt, vinegar, oil and sugar, and stir thoroughly. Allow to rest in the refrigerator for at least 1 day before serving.

MEDITERRANEAN BULGUR WHEAT, VEGETABLE & HERB SALAD

Makes

6

servings

4 cups coarse bulgur wheat
8 spring onions
2 sweet red peppers
1 jalapeño pepper
6 stems asparagus
Olive oil for brushing + ½ cup olive oil
1 bunch parsley, chopped
1 bunch mint, chopped
1 large purple onion, peeled and chopped
½ cup lemon juice
4 small carrots, finely chopped
Seeds of 1 pomegranate
Coarse salt, to taste
Ground black pepper, to taste

A note from the chef: This beautiful salad is sure to be the most colorful and exotic dish at the table. The bulgur wheat will need time to soak in the herb and vegetable flavors, so be sure to prepare this dish before the other items on your menu.

If you don't have the vegetables in the recipe in your refrigerator, don't worry! This recipe is so versatile that you can play with the flavors by adding or subtracting any vegetable or herb listed in the ingredients.

1. Preheat grill.
2. In a large covered bowl, soak the bulgur wheat in hot water for ½ hour. Rinse and drain.
3. Oil the grill grate. Brush the spring onions, red peppers, jalapeño pepper and asparagus with olive oil. Grill vegetables until lightly charred.
4. Using grilling tongs, remove vegetables from grill. Remove the stems and seeds from the peppers, clean and chop. Slice the asparagus and spring onions about ⅛-inch long.
5. Mix the bulgur wheat, spring onions, red peppers, jalapeño pepper and asparagus together with the parsley, mint, purple onion, lemon juice, ½ cup olive oil, carrots and pomegranate seeds in a bowl. Taste and adjust seasoning with salt and pepper. Allow salad to sit for 30 minutes before serving.

COUNTRY POTATO CAKES WITH YOGURT & GRILLED CHERRY TOMATOES

Makes
12
servings

1 bunch cherry tomatoes, on the stem
½ cup olive oil
12 medium-sized red potatoes
Coarse salt, to taste
Ground black pepper, to taste

For serving:
Goat's milk yogurt

1. Preheat grill.
2. Oil grill grate. Brush cherry tomatoes with olive oil and sear on the grill.
3. Peel and grate the potatoes. Place the grated potatoes in a colander, rinse and drain.
4. Place a 4- to 6-inch cast-iron skillet on the grill, or use a pancake ring of the desired diameter. Heat 1 teaspoon of the olive oil in the skillet.
5. Spoon grated potatoes into the skillet and fry the potato cake until golden and crispy, for a maximum of 5 minutes. Turn the potato cake and continue frying until both sides are the same color and texture. This is likely to happen well before 5 minutes pass, so it is important to check the potato cake periodically rather than setting a timer.
6. Remove the potato cake from the skillet and heat another teaspoon of olive oil in the skillet.
7. Repeat steps 5 and 6 until all the grated potatoes have been fried.
8. Using a thick barbecue mitt, remove skillet from grill. Transfer potato cakes to a serving dish and sprinkle them with salt and pepper to taste. Serve with a side of chilled goat's milk yogurt and the grilled tomatoes.

🔥 **A note from the chef:** These golden potato pancakes, topped with seasoned cherry tomatoes from the grill, are the epitome of summer comfort food. Country Potato Cakes are great on the side of fish and poultry, or they can stand alone as a hearty vegetarian option.

03
MEAT

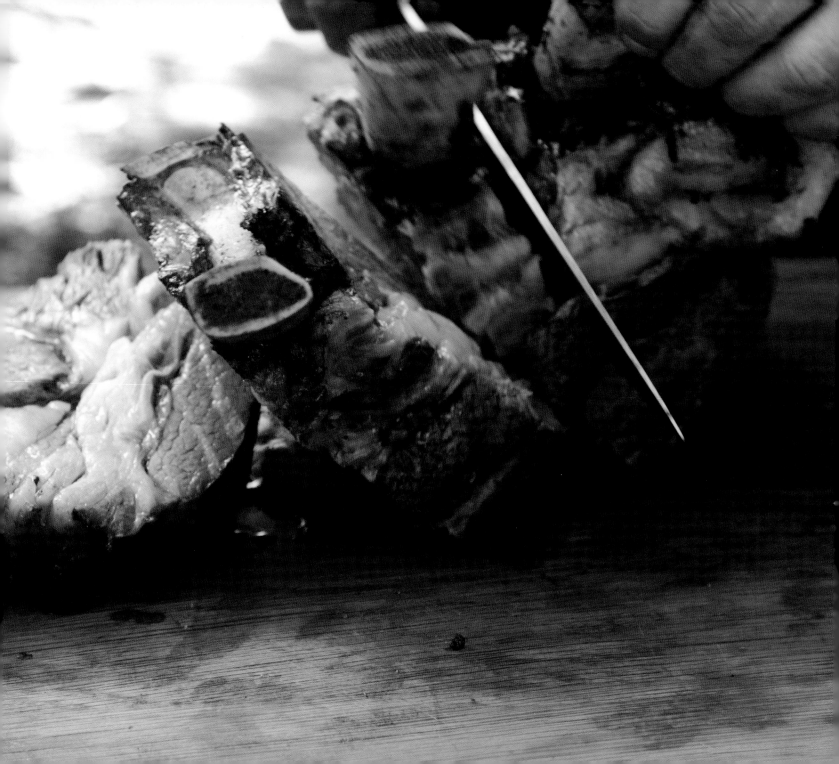

BURGER BASICS

The cut of meat you use in your burgers will greatly influence the flavor. I recommend using beef chuck or beef plate (or a mixture of both) for hamburgers. Ask your butcher to grind the meat twice for an exceptionally smooth burger patty. For healthier fare, substitute ground turkey for ground beef in any hamburger recipe.

GIANT HOME-STYLE HAMBURGER

Makes

4

servings

🔥 **A note from the chef:** This jumbo burger is a fun way to draw the entire family in for a shared meal. Serve it with your favorite condiments over a large bed of lettuce or on an oversized bun and split into quarters.

1 tablespoon olive oil
1 large onion, finely chopped
2 pounds finely ground beef
1 teaspoon coarse salt
1 teaspoon ground black pepper

For serving:
4 sesame seed hamburger buns, split
4 lettuce leaves
1 large tomato, sliced
Mayonnaise
Pickles

1. In a skillet over the grill, warm olive oil. Sauté the chopped onion until tender.
2. In a large bowl, combine the onion, ground beef, salt and pepper, and knead well until a smooth mixture is formed.
3. On a greased baking tray, form 4 giant burger patties from the ground beef mixture. Refrigerate for 1 hour.
4. Preheat grill.
5. Oil the grill grate. Transfer the patties to the grill by flipping the baking tray onto the grill. This should be done as close to the grill as possible to prevent the patties from separating.
6. Grill over a low flame for 3 minutes.
7. Flip the burger and grill for another 3 minutes, until juicy and medium-rare. Place the buns, cut-side down, on the grill to toast during the last minute that the burger is cooking. Serve the burgers on the toasted buns with lettuce, tomato, mayonnaise and pickles.

HAMBURGER NAPOLITANO

Makes

5

servings

🔥 A note from the chef: Not sure if you're in the mood for classic American or Italian cuisine? Have both! Zingy pesto and fresh mozzarella atop American beef are sure to stimulate every taste bud in your mouth! This burger can become true gourmet with the simple addition of grilled artichoke or cherry tomatoes.

1 tablespoon olive oil
1 large onion, finely chopped
2 pounds finely ground beef
1 teaspoon coarse salt
½ teaspoon ground black pepper

For serving:
5 sesame seed hamburger buns, split
3 tablespoons Pesto (page 22)
3½ ounces mozzarella cheese, coarsely grated

1. In a skillet over the grill, warm olive oil. Sauté the chopped onion until tender.
2. In a large bowl, combine the onions with the ground beef, salt and pepper and knead well until a smooth mixture is formed.
3. Shape the ground meat mixture into 5 flat patties. Refrigerate for 1 hour.
4. Preheat grill.
5. Oil the grill grate. Grill the patties over a low flame for 3 minutes.
6. Flip the burgers with a spatula and grill for another 3 minutes, until juicy and medium-rare. Place the buns, cut-side down, on the grill to toast during the last minute that the burgers are cooking.
7. Spread Pesto on the toasted side of the burger buns. Place the burgers on the toasted buns and sprinkle the burgers with mozzarella cheese. Serve immediately.

SURF & TURF BURGERS

Makes

5

servings

2 pounds finely ground beef chuck or beef plate
1 tablespoon coarse salt
½ teaspoon ground black pepper
5 ounces chopped shrimp and calamari mixture
1 teaspoon thyme

For serving:
5 sesame seed hamburger buns, split
5 lettuce leaves
1 large tomato, sliced
Mayonnaise
Pickles

🔥 A note from the chef: Chopped seafood adds sweet and buttery undertones to this burger and also produces a scintillating aroma on the grill, for a fully rounded sensory experience. If you want to call extra attention to this burger's sweetness, serve it with a piece of melted sharp cheddar.

1. In a large bowl, combine the ground beef, salt, pepper, chopped seafood and thyme. Mix until smooth. Set the mixture aside for 1 hour to absorb the flavors.
2. Preheat grill.
3. Divide mixture into 5 flat patties.
4. Oil the grill grate. Grill the patties over a low flame for 3 minutes.
5. Flip the burgers with a spatula and grill for another 3 minutes, until juicy and medium-rare. Place the buns, cut-side down, on the grill to toast during the last minute that the burgers are cooking.
6. Using grilling tongs, remove burgers from grill. Serve the burgers on the toasted buns with lettuce, tomato, mayonnaise and pickles.

FIESTA BURGER

Makes

4

servings

🔥 **A note from the chef:** Crushed tortilla chips add color, texture and flavor to these south-of-the border burgers. The Fiesta Burger is best accompanied by an assortment of taco toppings like pico de gallo, fresh avocado and sour cream.

2 pounds ground beef
5 ounces (approximately 1 cup) tortilla chips, roughly chopped or crushed
2 tablespoons Tabasco® Chipotle sauce

For serving:
4 sesame seed hamburger buns, split
Taco toppings

1. In a large bowl, combine the ground beef, tortilla chips and Tabasco® sauce together. Thoroughly knead until smooth.
2. Shape the ground meat mixture into 4 flat patties.
3. Refrigerate for 1 hour.
4. Preheat grill.
5. Oil the grill grate. Grill the patties over a low flame for 3 minutes.
6. Flip the burgers with a spatula and grill for another 3 minutes, until juicy and medium-rare. Place the buns, cut-side down, on the grill to toast during the last minute that the burgers are cooking.
7. Place the burgers on the toasted buns, top each burger with taco toppings of your choice, and serve immediately.

FRESH HERB DRUMSTICK SKEWERS

Makes

8

servings

🔥 **A note from the chef:** Fresh cilantro, parsley and mint unite in this finger-licking drumstick. The chicken's spectacular blast of flavor makes it an ideal entrée, salad topper or lunch meat.

For the Marinade:
1 bunch cilantro, chopped
1 bunch parsley, chopped
1 bunch mint, chopped
Coarse salt, to taste
Ground black pepper, to taste
½ cup lemon juice
½ cup olive oil
12 garlic cloves, crushed

16 drumsticks, with bones and skin

1. **Prepare the Marinade:** In a bowl, combine the cilantro, parsley, mint, salt, pepper, lemon juice, olive oil and garlic.
2. Add the drumsticks to the marinade and soak for 2 to 8 hours, depending on the desired concentration of flavor.
3. Preheat grill.
4. Remove the drumsticks from the Marinade and skewer them from the meatier end.
5. Oil the grill grate. Place the skewers over a low fire and sear on one side for about 4 minutes. Turn and sear on the other side until the chicken meat is no longer pink at the bone and when pierced with a fork the juices run clear.
6. Using grilling tongs, transfer skewers to dinner plates. Serve immediately.

GRILLED STUFFED CHICKEN

Makes

6

servings

🔥 A note from the chef: The chicken and rice in this dish have a unique symbiotic relationship whereby they season and enhance each other's flavor. Rice should be al dente when stuffed into the bird to prevent overcooking.

For the Marinade:
½ cup olive oil
½ teaspoon coarse salt
½ teaspoon ground black pepper
1 tablespoon sumac
2 garlic cloves, crushed

1 medium-sized whole chicken, approximately 3½ pounds

For the Filling:
2 white onions, chopped
½ cup olive oil
2 cups short grain rice, soaked in water for ½ hour
2 cups water
½ cup toasted pine nuts
1 bunch dill, chopped
1 bunch parsley, chopped
1 bunch mint, chopped
Coarse salt, to taste
Ground black pepper, to taste

1. Preheat grill.
2. **Prepare the Marinade:** In a mixing bowl, combine the olive oil, salt, pepper, sumac and garlic.
3. Rub the chicken all over with the Marinade.
4. **Prepare the Filling:** Warm a skillet on the grill and sauté the chopped onions in the olive oil until tender.
5. Drain the rice in a colander and cook in water over a low flame for 20 minutes. The rice does not need to be completely cooked. Add the pine nuts, dill, parsley, mint, salt and pepper to the rice. Mix with a fork.
6. Allow the rice to cool and spoon the Filling into the chicken. Close the opening of the cavity with a toothpick.
7. **If using a charcoal grill:** Wrap the chicken in several layers of aluminum foil. The chicken should be completely covered. Insert the chicken into the coals on the grill. The chicken should be under the grill grate. Cover chicken on all sides with coal embers. Cook chicken for 2 hours, until the chicken meat is no longer pink at the bone and when pierced with a fork, the juices run clear.
8. **If using a gas grill:** Oil the grill grate. Place the chicken on the coolest side of the grill, breast up. Using grilling tongs, rotate the chicken after about 40 minutes and recover. After a total of 80 minutes, pierce the thickest part of the chicken with a knife, and grill until the juices run clear.
9. Using a thick barbecue mitt, transfer the chicken to a carving board and allow to rest for 10 minutes. Cut the chicken for serving and serve hot.

PATAGONIAN GRILLED CHICKEN BREASTS

Makes

6

servings

🔥 **A note from the chef:** Herb-based Argentinean Chimichurri salsa is a piquant companion for various kinds of grilled meats. Chicken, pork and red meat all benefit from a dollop of Chimichurri. You can even use it as a hamburger topping.

For the Chimichurri Salsa:
1 bunch parsley, chopped
1 bunch cilantro, chopped
1 red chili pepper, chopped
10 garlic cloves, chopped
Coarse salt, to taste
Ground black pepper, to taste
½ cup sunflower seed oil
¼ cup white wine vinegar
Juice from 1 lemon

3 boneless chicken breasts
Olive oil

1. **Prepare the Chimichurri Salsa:** In a mixing bowl, combine the parsley, cilantro, chili pepper, garlic, salt, black pepper, sunflower oil, vinegar and lemon juice. Store in a jar. It is recommended to do this step at least 1 day in advance of grilling the chicken to allow the salsa's flavor to develop.
2. Preheat grill.
3. Butterfly the chicken breasts into a scaloppini cut, approximately ½-inch thick.
4. Brush with olive oil, and oil the grill grate. Grill chicken over a medium fire and sear on one side, for about 4 minutes. Turn and sear on the other side until the juices run clear when pierced with a fork.
5. Using a thick barbecue mitt, transfer the chicken breasts to a carving board, and allow to rest for 5 to 10 minutes.
6. Cut for serving. Transfer the chicken breasts to dinner plates, spoon some Chimichurri Salsa on top of the chicken breasts, and serve hot.

CRISPY SALTED CORNISH GAME HEN

Makes
10
servings

🔥 **A note from the chef:** The simple flavors in this dish highlight the unique texture that results from the double-cooking process. Enjoy the crispy texture of fried chicken without ever having to dip your bird into a deep-fryer.

4 Cornish game hens, about 1½ pounds each, butterflied
½ cup olive oil
Coarse salt, to taste
Ground black pepper, to taste

1. Preheat grill.
2. Brush the game hens with olive oil. Season with salt and pepper.
3. Arrange the hens in a baking tray and place on the grill. Close the grill cover and cook for 20 to 30 minutes.
4. Remove the game hens from the baking tray, butterfly them, and place them on the grill for another 3 to 4 minutes, until the skin is crispy.
5. Transfer the game hens to a carving board and allow to rest for 5 to 10 minutes. Carve, transfer to dinner plates and serve hot.

CHICKEN SATAY SKEWERS WITH PEANUT SAUCE

Makes

6

servings

🔥 **A note from the chef:** Aromatic Chicken Satay Skewers are a Thai classic featuring the bold flavors of ginger and crushed coriander. Spice lovers can add a pinch of cayenne pepper for extra zing.

For the Marinade:
2 shallots, finely chopped
1 clove garlic, crushed
1½ pieces of ginger, crushed
3 tablespoons light soy sauce
½ tablespoon brown sugar
1 heaping tablespoon green curry paste
2 tablespoons lime juice

2 pounds chicken breast, sliced about 1½ inches wide

For the Satay Peanut Sauce:
⅓ cup peanut oil
2 shallots, chopped
1 tablespoon light soy sauce
2 garlic cloves, crushed
3 green onion stalks, chopped
½ cup coconut milk
3 tablespoons peanut butter

1. **Prepare the Marinade:** In a large bowl, combine the shallots, garlic, ginger, soy sauce, sugar, curry paste and lime juice. Add the chicken cutlets. Cover the bowl with plastic wrap and place in the refrigerator to marinate for a minimum of 3 hours. It is preferable to marinate the chicken overnight.
2. Preheat grill.
3. **Prepare the Satay Peanut Sauce:** Place a pot on the grill, warm the peanut oil, and sauté the shallots. Add the soy sauce, garlic, green onion stalks, coconut milk and peanut butter, and cook until sauce reduces.
4. Thread 1 chicken cutlet onto each wooden skewer. Oil the grill grate. Grill the chicken for 2 minutes on each side. Drizzle with Satay Peanut Sauce.
5. Using grilling tongs, transfer skewers to dinner plates. Serve immediately.

RED FIRE WINGS

Makes

4

servings

🔥 A note from the chef: To ensure maximum impact of the spices in this recipe, be sure to remove the wingtips and fat, and clean the wings well.
I recommend saving some of the marinade for brushing the wings while grilling.

For the Marinade:
1 tablespoon hot paprika
1 tablespoon sweet paprika
8 garlic cloves, crushed
Coarse salt, to taste
Ground black pepper, to taste
½ cup olive oil

12 chicken wings, about 2 pounds

1. **Prepare the Marinade:** In a large mixing bowl, combine the hot paprika, sweet paprika, garlic, salt, pepper and olive oil in a bowl. Add the chicken wings and set aside for 1 hour.
2. Preheat grill. Skewer the chicken wings onto a metal skewer, arranging 4 wings on each skewer, alternating between drumettes and wingettes. Set aside half the marinade to use during grilling. Oil the grill grate. Place wings on grill and sear on each side, for about 5 minutes. Brush the wings with Marinade and continue to grill, until the skin is crispy and the juices run clear.
3. Using grilling tongs, transfer the wings to dinner plates and serve immediately.

CURRY-MINT CHICKEN WING SKEWERS

Makes
4
servings

🔥 A note from the chef: Make the color and flavor schemes of this recipe even more robust by adding cherry tomatoes and green pepper to the ends of your skewers.

For the Marinade:
1 cup goat's milk yogurt
1 tablespoon yellow curry paste
1 tablespoon dry mint
1 teaspoon coarse salt

12 chicken wings, about 2 pounds

1. **Prepare the Marinade:** In a large mixing bowl, combine the goat milk yogurt, curry paste, mint and salt. Add the chicken wings. Set aside for 1 hour.
2. Preheat grill.
3. Skewer the chicken wings onto a metal skewer, arranging 4 wings on each skewer, alternating between drumettes and wingettes. Set aside half the marinade to use during grilling.
4. Oil the grill grate. Place the wings on the grill and sear on one side, for about 5 minutes. Turn and sear on the other side, for about 5 more minutes. Brush the wings all over with Marinade and continue to grill, until the skin is crispy and the juices run clear.
5. Using grilling tongs, transfer the wings to dinner plates and serve immediately.

LAMB-PISTACHIO SAUSAGE

Makes

12

sausages

🔥 **A note from the chef:** If you're a sausage enthusiast, this recipe for homemade sausages is the perfect way to share your passion with your guests. Preparing sausage links at home will require some advanced preparation and the help of a sausage stuffer. Natural or synthetic sausage casings can be ordered from your local butcher or online, and should be delivered at least two days before your cookout. If preparing sausage links at home is too laborious, use the same recipe to make succulent sausage patties. Or make sensational sliders by serving the patties on mini-buns with crumbled goat's milk feta cheese.

3 pounds ground lamb and veal rib meat
2 tablespoons Chef's Pepper Marinade [page 22]
1 tablespoon coarse salt
½ teaspoon black pepper
1 cup pistachios, shelled and chopped
1 cup parsley, chopped
½ cup water

4 feet natural or synthetic sausage casing
Twine

1. In a large mixing bowl, combine the ground meat, Chef's Pepper Marinade, salt, pepper, pistachios, parsley and water together. If you plan to grind your meat at home, it is best to season before grinding.
2. Transfer the mixture to a meat grinder with a sausage-stuffing attachment and thread sausage casing onto the attachment. Tie a string at the end of the casing.
3. Fill the sausage casing with the ground meat mixture, taking care not to overstuff the casing. Divide the sausages into 4-inch links by pinching the casing with your fingers until the meat is pushed to either side of your fingers, creating a hollow section in the casing. Tie twine around the empty section of casing. Use a toothpick to poke several holes into each sausage so that excess air can escape.
4. Store the sausages in the refrigerator for at least 5 hours and up to 2 days before grilling.
5. Preheat grill.
6. Parboil the sausages in 180°F water before grilling. Remove the sausages from the water when you see the fat has liquefied inside the casing.
7. Oil the grill grate. Place the sausages on the grill grate or griddle, on a medium-hot fire. Grill the sausages, turning once, until lightly charred on both sides and fully cooked, for about 6 to 8 minutes in total.
8. Using grilling tongs, transfer sausages to dinner plates. Serve immediately.

PORK SUMMER SAUSAGES

Makes
15
sausages

🔥 **A note from the chef:** This classic sausage recipe is a fail-proof crowd pleaser that also provides an excellent canvas for experimentation. For sweeter sausages, try adding ground apples and dates.
If you like your sausage spicy, add ½ teaspoon of hot paprika or cayenne pepper to the mix.

3 pounds pork, preferably shoulder meat
1½ tablespoons fine grain salt
1 tablespoon white pepper
2 tablespoons dry thyme
2 tablespoons garlic powder
1 teaspoon crushed coriander seeds
½ cup water
5 feet synthetic sausage casing
Twine
15 hot dog buns
11 oz. sauerkraut, drained
Ketchup
Mustard

1. Chop the meat into 1½- to 2-inch cubes, or pass through a meat grinder. If you don't have a meat grinder at home, ask the butcher to grind the pork meat for you.
2. In a bowl, thoroughly mix the pork meat, salt, white pepper, thyme, garlic powder, coriander and water. If you plan to grind your meat at home, it is best to season before grinding.
3. Transfer the mixture to a meat grinder with a sausage-stuffing attachment and thread sausage casing onto the attachment. Tie a string at the end of the casing.
4. Fill the sausage casing with the ground pork, taking care not to overstuff the casing. Divide the sausages into 4-inch links by pinching the casing with your fingers until the meat is pushed to either side of your fingers, creating a hollow section in the casing. Tie twine around the empty section of casing. Use a toothpick to poke several holes into each sausage so that excess air can escape.
5. Store the sausages in the refrigerator for at least 5 hours and up to 2 days before grilling.
6. Preheat grill.
7. Parboil the sausages in 180°F water before grilling. Remove the sausages from the water when you see the fat has liquefied inside the casing.
8. Oil the grill grate. Place the sausages on the grill grate or griddle, on a medium-hot fire. Grill the sausages, turning once, until lightly charred on both sides and fully cooked, for about 6 to 8 minutes in total.
9. Using a grilling tong, transfer sausages to buns. Add sauerkraut, ketchup and mustard to taste and serve immediately.

ROMANIAN-STYLE KABOBS

Makes

8

servings

🔥 A note from the chef: These straight-forward kabobs are great as a patty or on a skewer. Serve over a mound of freshly prepared Romanian Eggplant Salad (page 68).

3½ pounds finely ground beef
10 garlic cloves, crushed
1 tablespoon coarse salt
1 teaspoon ground black pepper
1 tablespoon baking soda, dissolved into ½ cup soda water

1. In a large bowl, combine the ground beef, garlic, salt, pepper and baking soda, and knead until the mixture is smooth. Set the meat mixture aside for ½ hour.
2. Preheat grill.
3. Shape meat mixture into thick, oblong kabobs.
4. Oil the grill grate. Grill over a very low flame, turning every 2 minutes until the kabobs are evenly cooked.
5. Using grilling tongs, transfer kabobs to dinner plates. Serve immediately.

OLD-WORLD PORK KABOBS

Makes

6

servings

🔥 A note from the chef: Make an entire meal on an extra long skewer by alternating meat and vegetables. Another option is to sweeten your kabobs with some pineapple cubes.

3 pounds pork shoulder, cut into 1½-inch cubes
1 tablespoon oregano, mixed with 1 tablespoon salt

1. Preheat grill.
2. Skewer the cubes of pork onto a wide metal skewer. Sprinkle some of the oregano-salt mixture onto the kabobs.
3. Oil the grill grate. Grill kabobs over a very low flame, turning every 2 minutes until they are evenly cooked. Scatter more of the oregano-salt mixture onto the meat each time you turn the skewer.
4. Using grilling tongs, transfer kabobs to dinner plates. Serve immediately.

NEW YORK STRIP STEAK WITH DOWNTOWN MANHATTAN SAUCE

Makes

2

servings

🔥 **A note from the chef:** Just like Manhattan, you can find a little bit of everything in this anything-but-ordinary strip steak recipe.

For the Manhattan Sauce:

15 cherry tomatoes
2 large onions, sliced in rings
1 red chili pepper
Olive oil
⅓ cup brown sugar
½ cup sherry vinegar
1 tablespoon crushed coriander seeds
Coarse salt, to taste
Ground black pepper, to taste
1 tablespoon honey or maple syrup

2 New York strip steaks, about 16 ounces each

1. Preheat grill.
2. **Prepare the Manhattan Sauce:** Brush the cherry tomatoes, onion and chili pepper with olive oil, and grill until lightly seared. Transfer vegetables to a warm skillet on the grill.
3. Add sugar, vinegar, coriander, salt and pepper to taste. Stir and bring to a gentle boil. Allow the mixture to simmer on low heat for 5 minutes.
4. Transfer mixture to a bowl and purée with a hand blender. Add honey or maple syrup to thicken the sauce.
5. Oil the grill grate. Brush steaks with olive oil and grill the steaks on one side, 5 minutes for rare or 7 minutes for medium-rare. Turn and cook for 4 minutes more, or until steaks yield slightly to the touch.
6. Remove the steaks from the grill, transfer to dinner plates, and drizzle with warm Manhattan Sauce. Serve immediately.

MARINATED LAMB CHOPS

Makes
6
servings

For the Marinade:
½ cup olive oil
Juice from ½ lemon
Coarse salt, to taste
Ground black pepper, to taste
1 tablespoon crushed dried oregano
4 stems thyme
2-3 garlic cloves, crushed

2½-pound rack of lamb, about 8 to 12 chops, sliced into pairs

🔥 A note from the chef: These heavenly chops are a must for every cookout! Pair your chops with delectable Grilled Beets with Cool Greek Tzatziki Sauce (page 60) or with Grilled Vegetable Antipasti (page 53).

1. **Prepare the Marinade:** In a large bowl, combine the olive oil, lemon juice, salt, pepper, oregano, thyme and garlic. Add the lamb chops and set aside for 1 hour.
2. Preheat grill.
3. Oil the grill grate. Grill the lamb chops over a low flame or on a raised grill gate for 3 minutes on each side for rare, or 4 minutes for medium-rare.
4. Remove the chops from the grill and allow to rest for 5 minutes. Transfer each pair of chops to a dinner plate.

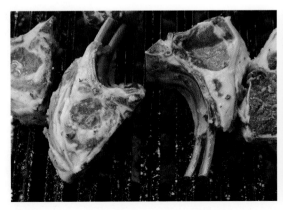

SMOKED ITALIAN PORCHETTA PORK

Makes

10

servings

🔥 **A note from the chef:** This rustic dish takes its rich flavor from slow cooking seasoned livers inside a prime cut pork loin. Bring even more authenticity to this traditional favorite by serving it the way the Italians do—on a toasted baguette or ciabatta bread.

Storage instructions: Smoked Italian Porchetta Pork can be stored in the refrigerator in a plastic wrap poked with holes for up to 1 week, or in the freezer in a freezer storage container for up to 2 months.

7½–8 pounds boneless pork loin or shoulder, butterflied and flattened
2 cups salt, dissolved into 4½ cups water

For the Filling:
1 tablespoon olive oil
2–3 white onions, chopped
½ pound chicken livers, cubed
1 cup red wine
Coarse salt, to taste
Ground black pepper, to taste
2 tablespoons dry ground oregano

Twine

1. In a large bowl, soak the pork in the salt water solution for 1 to 2 nights.
2. Preheat grill and prepare smoker.
3. Prepare the filling immediately before smoking the pork loin. In a frying pan on the grill, warm the olive oil. Add the onions and fry until tender. Add the chicken livers and fry until the livers are lightly seared.
4. Add red wine and bring to a boil. Cook for 5 minutes until the liquid has evaporated. Season with salt, pepper and oregano.
5. Spoon the filling onto one end of the pork loin and roll it. Hold the roll together with twine.
6. Cook the pork in a smoker at a temperature of 200°F to 225°F for 3 to 4 hours.
7. Transfer the pork to a carving board and allow to rest for 10 minutes. Cut for serving. Transfer to dinner plates and serve hot.

MELTING-OFF-THE-BONE SMOKED CHICKEN

Makes 6 servings

🔥 A note from the chef: True to its name, this slow-cooking recipe produces tender chicken that falls right off the bone—no knife required! Stick a halved and pitted apricot, or a halved orange inside the chicken to infuse your bird with fruit flavors.

For the Marinade:
1 cup sunflower seed oil
4 garlic cloves, crushed
1 tablespoon sweet paprika
1 teaspoon coarse salt
1 teaspoon ground black pepper

1 medium-sized whole chicken, about 3½-4 pounds

1. **Prepare the Marinade:** In a large bowl, mix the sunflower oil, garlic, sweet paprika, salt and black pepper.
2. Thoroughly rub the spice mixture into the chicken, inside and out.
3. Truss the chicken at the legs and wings. Place the chicken in the marinade and cover the bowl with plastic wrap. Let the chicken marinate overnight.
4. Prepare the smoker.
5. Cook the chicken in a smoker at a temperature of 175°F to 250°F for 3 to 4 hours.
6. Transfer the chicken to a carving board and allow to rest for 10 minutes. Cut for serving. Transfer to dinner plates and serve hot.

Storage instructions: Melting-off-the-Bone Smoked Chicken can be stored in the refrigerator in a plastic wrap poked with holes for up to 1 week, or in the freezer in a freezer storage container for up to 2 months.

SMOKED TURKEY

For the Marinade:
2 cans dark beer
1 cup pure maple syrup

1 boneless turkey breast with skin, about 5-6 pounds,
  split in half and tied with twine

🔥 **A note from the chef:** Make your co-workers swoon over your lunch by bringing an overstuffed home-cooked turkey sandwich to the office. Turkey is an exceptional canvas for sauces and spreads—be adventurous and swap mustard for a spoonful of Olive Tapenade Dip (page 33) on your next sandwich.

1. **Prepare the Marinade:** In a large bowl, combine the dark beer and maple syrup.
2. Place the turkey breast in the Marinade, cover, and soak in the refrigerator overnight. Turn the turkey at least twice during the soaking process.
3. Prepare the smoker.
4. Cook the turkey in the smoker at a temperature of 175°F to 250°F for 3 hours.
5. Transfer the turkey to a carving board and allow to rest for 10 minutes. Carve, transfer to dinner plates and serve hot.

Storage instructions: Smoked Turkey can be stored in the refrigerator in a plastic wrap poked with holes for up to 1 week, or in the freezer in a freezer storage container for up to 2 months.

SMOKED BEEF SPARE RIBS

Makes
20
servings

🔥 **A note from the chef:** Serve this indulgent finger food smothered in your favorite barbecue sauce over a bed of leafy lettuce.

6½ pounds Flanken-style short ribs, 2- to 3-inches in length
2 tablespoons crushed coriander seeds
2 tablespoons coarse salt
2 tablespoons ground black pepper

1. Prepare the smoker.
2. Season the meat with the crushed coriander.
3. Place the ribs on the lowest shelf of a smoker heated to 200°F to 225°F for 1 hour. Turn the ribs 3 times during the smoking process.
4. Cover the ribs in aluminum foil and return to the smoker on a higher rack for an additional 3 hours.
5. Using grilling tongs, remove the ribs from the smoker and allow to rest for 10 minutes. Season the ribs with salt and pepper. Cut for serving. Transfer to dinner plates and serve hot.

Storage instructions: Smoked Beef Spare Ribs can be stored in the refrigerator in a plastic wrap poked with holes for up to 1 week, or in the freezer in a freezer storage container for up to 2 months

SMOKED RIB-EYE STEAK

Makes
20
servings

🔥 **A note from the chef:** It's important to avoid seasoning your steaks with salt and pepper before placing them in the smoker. When smoked, salt and pepper in particular tend to leave a burnt taste in the meat, so it's always best to apply salt and pepper after smoking.

11-12 pounds fresh aged rib-eye steak, with bone
½ cup olive oil
2 tablespoons fresh chopped rosemary or thyme
2 tablespoons coarse salt
2 tablespoons ground black pepper

1. Prepare the smoker.
2. Brush the steak with olive oil, and season with rosemary or thyme.
3. Place the steaks on the lowest shelf of a smoker at 200°F to 225°F for 1 hour. Turn the steaks 3 times during the smoking process.
4. Cover the steaks in aluminum foil and return to the smoker on a higher rack for an additional 3 hours.
5. Remove the steaks from the smoker and allow to rest for 10 minutes before serving. Season the steaks with salt and pepper, slice and serve hot.

Storage instructions: Smoked Rib-Eye Steak can be stored in the refrigerator in a plastic wrap poked with holes for up to 1 week, or in the freezer in a freezer storage container for up to 2 months.

SMOKED PORK LOIN

Makes

10

servings

🔥 **A note from the chef:** This succulent pork dish's fragrance and full-bodied combination of spices may just have you trading in your traditional holiday ham recipe. Make the pork loin match any season through careful side dish selection. In summer, serve it with refreshing Grilled Artichokes with Fresh Yogurt and Mint (page 57). For a wintry meal, serve Everybody's Favorite Smashed Potatoes (page 50).

For the Marinade:
½ cup salt
¼ cup ground black pepper
6 garlic cloves, whole
6 allspice peppercorns
6 juniper berries
10 bay leaves
4 cups water
1 bottle pale beer

2 cuts of boneless pork tenderloin with skin, about
   3½ pounds each

1. **Prepare the Marinade:** In a large bowl, combine the salt, pepper, garlic, peppercorns, juniper berries, bay leaves, water and beer.
2. Place the pork loin in the Marinade, cover, and soak in the refrigerator for at least 2 days. I recommend placing some kind of weight on the meat to ensure it stays completely immersed in the liquid.
3. Prepare the smoker.
4. Remove the pork loin from the Marinade, pat dry, and smoke the meat at 250°F for 3-5 hours.
5. Using a thick barbecue mitt, remove pork from smoker. Transfer the pork loin to a carving board and allow to rest for 10 minutes. Cut for serving. Transfer to dinner plates and serve hot.

Storage instructions: Smoked Pork Loin can be stored in the refrigerator in a plastic wrap poked with holes for up to 1 week, or in the freezer in a freezer storage container for up to 2 months.

SMOKED PORK SHORT RIBS

Makes

4

servings

🔥 **A note from the chef:** Don't be fooled by the seemingly simple seasonings employed in this recipe. Using the bare minimum of salt, pepper and thyme to season your ribs is the key to highlighting the rich, woody flavors gained through smoke cooking.

2½–3 pounds short ribs
½ cup olive oil

For serving:
2 tablespoons coarse salt
1 tablespoon ground black pepper
2 tablespoons fresh thyme, chopped

1. Prepare smoker.
2. Brush the ribs with olive oil.
3. Cook the pork in the smoker at a temperature of 200°F to 225°F for 3 hours.
4. Remove ribs from the smoker and season with salt, pepper and thyme. Allow to rest for 10 minutes. Serve hot.

Storage instructions: Smoked Pork Short Ribs can be stored in the refrigerator in a plastic wrap poked with holes for up to 1 week, or in the freezer in a freezer storage container for up to 2 months.

SMOKED PORK RIBS

Makes

4

servings

🔥 **A note from the chef:** Nothing says summer like slow-cooked pork ribs. To sweeten your ribs, brush them with a touch of apricot jam after smoking and throw them on the grill for a minute to lock in the flavor.

For the Brine:
2 quarts water
¾ cup salt
⅓ cup garlic powder
⅓ cup white pepper

3-pound rack of pork neck bones

1. **Prepare the Brine:** In a large bowl, combine the water, salt, garlic powder and pepper. Let the ribs marinate in the Brine for 2 days in the refrigerator. I recommend placing some kind of weight on the meat to ensure that it stays completely immersed in the liquid.
2. Prepare the smoker.
3. Smoke the pork at 250°F for 4 hours.
4. Using grilling tongs, remove the ribs from the smoker and allow to rest for 10 minutes. Cut for serving. Transfer to dinner plates and serve hot.

Storage instructions: Smoked Pork Ribs can be stored in the refrigerator in a plastic wrap poked with holes for up to 1 week, or in the freezer in a freezer storage container for up to 2 months.

04
FISH
&
SEAFOOD

SEARED WASABI TUNA

Makes **2** servings

A note from the chef: Nothing stirs the senses quite like the sharp tingle of wasabi spice, a Japanese horseradish. Wasabi emits a distinctive heat that is not for the fainthearted, so it is best to use the spice in conjunction with sweet ingredients to balance the sting.

For the Wasabi Sauce:
2 tablespoons peanut butter
⅓ cup sunflower seed oil
2 tablespoons mirin
1 teaspoon wasabi paste

1¼ pounds fresh tuna fillet, divided into two 10-ounce pieces
Olive oil

1. Preheat grill.
2. **Prepare the Wasabi Sauce:** In a bowl, mix the peanut butter, sunflower oil, mirin and wasabi paste.
3. Brush the fish fillets with olive oil. Oil the grill grate. Place the fillets on the grill grate and close the grill cover. Grill fish for 2 minutes on each side.
4. Remove fish from the grill. Transfer to dinner plates and serve with the Wasabi Sauce on the side.

GIANT SALT-BAKED WHITE FISH

Makes **8** to **10** servings

A note from the chef: The flavor packed into this fish is rivaled only by its size. Use a meaty fish like Amberjack or Red Snapper for best results.

6½ pounds coarse salt
1 whole fish, about 5-5½ pounds, gutted, cleaned and scaled
1 cup water

1. Preheat grill.
2. Cover the bottom of a large metal baking dish with half the salt. Place the fish over the salt, and cover it with the remaining salt.
3. Using a spoon, gently sprinkle the water over the salt. Place the baking dish on the grill over a low flame and close the grill cover. Bake for 20 minutes.
4. Remove the baking dish from the grill and carefully break the salt with an ice pick or a knife.
5. Separate the skin from the fish and serve hot.

Giant Salt-Baked White Fish

BAKED SALMON WITH MUSTARD AIOLI

Makes

6

servings

🔥 **A note from the chef**: This method for preparing salmon traps all the fish's liquids to produce succulent, juicy fillets. Try serving it with a side of Grilled Cherry Tomatoes with Thyme (page 66).

6 skinless salmon fillets, about 3¼ pounds

For the Mustard Aioli:
1 cup olive oil
½ cup vinegar
Juice from ½ lemon
Coarse salt, to taste
Ground black pepper, to taste
2 tablespoons mustard
1 small jar capers, strained
3 eggs

For serving:
1 bunch tarragon, finely chopped

1. Preheat grill.
2. Place the salmon fillets on a greased metal baking tray. Cover the tray with aluminum foil.
3. Place the tray on the grill grate and close the grill cover. Cook over medium-low heat for 20 minutes.
4. **Prepare the Mustard Aioli:** In a bowl, combine the olive oil, vinegar, lemon juice, salt, pepper, mustard, capers and eggs. Set aside.
5. Remove the aluminum foil and bake the salmon fillets for an additional 7 to 10 minutes.
6. Using a thick barbecue mitt, remove baking tray from grill and transfer salmon fillets to dinner plates. Drizzle with Mustard Aioli. Garnish with chopped tarragon and serve.

JUMBO SHRIMP SKEWERS WITH GINGER SAUCE

Makes

4

servings

🔥 **A note from the chef:** Whether served as an appetizer or entrée, these zesty seafood skewers always fly off the plate.

16-20 jumbo shrimps, peeled and deveined
4 limes, quartered

For the Ginger Sauce:
½ cup olive oil
Juice from 1 lemon
1½-inch piece of ginger, grated
Coarse salt, to taste
Ground black pepper, to taste

1. Preheat grill.
2. Skewer the shrimp and limes onto wide skewers.
3. **Prepare the Ginger Sauce:** In a bowl, mix the olive oil, lemon juice, ginger, salt and pepper. Brush Ginger Sauce onto the skewers.
4. Oil the grill grate. Place the skewers on a hot grill and cook for 2 minutes on each side, until grill marks appear.
5. Transfer the skewers to dinner plates. Serve hot.

GRILLED LOBSTER WITH CHESTNUT BUTTER

Makes

4

servings

4 lobsters, about 1 pound each
Olive oil

For the Chestnut Butter:
1 cup softened chestnuts (vacuum packed, or fresh,
  steamed or roasted)
¼ cup butter, room temperature
4 garlic cloves, crushed
Coarse salt, to taste
Ground black pepper, to taste

For serving:
½ bunch dill, chopped

♦ **A note from the chef:** If you are preparing food for a special occasion, grilled lobster is the perfect way to say "We're celebrating!" Create an extra air of festivity by serving lobster with a sparkling glass of champagne

1. Preheat grill.
2. Immerse the lobsters in a large pot of boiling water for 3 to 4 minutes until the color of the shells changes to deep red.
3. Remove the lobsters from the water and split each in half, lengthwise.
4. Brush olive oil over the lobster meat. Oil the grill grate. Place the lobsters on the grill grate, meat-side down, for 3 minutes.
5. **Prepare the Chestnut Butter:** In a metal bowl, use a spoon to mash the chestnuts into the butter. Add garlic, salt and pepper to taste. Place the bowl on the grill grate and heat the Chestnut Butter for 3 minutes.
6. Using grilling tongs, remove the lobsters from the grill and transfer to dinner plates. Drizzle generously with Chestnut Butter and sprinkle with dill. Serve hot.

HERB-GRILLED SEA BASS

Makes
6
servings

🔥 **A note from the chef:** Stuffing fish is a superb method for infusing flavor into every bite. Those who are squeamish about whole fish can cook a fillet, with the filling on top, in aluminum foil.

6 whole sea bass, about ¾ pounds each, gutted and cleaned
1 cup olive oil
Coarse salt, to taste
Ground black pepper, to taste
3 tomatoes, thinly sliced
2 lemons, thinly sliced
12 garlic cloves, peeled
6 sprigs of rosemary

For serving:
4 lemons, halved

1. Preheat grill.
2. Brush the fish with olive oil and season with salt and pepper.
3. Stuff the fish cavity with tomato slices, lemon slices, garlic cloves and rosemary.
4. Oil the grill grate. Place the fish on the grill grate and grill over a low flame.
5. Turn the fish when it can be easily separated from the grate. If the fish sticks to the grate, continue grilling for an additional 2 minutes and then turn. Grill for an additional 5 minutes after turning.
6. Squeeze fresh lemon over the fish a moment before removing the fish from the grill. Transfer the fish to dinner plates. Serve immediately.

SHRIMP & SCALLOP CITRUS SALAD

Makes

4

servings

🔥 **A note from the chef:** This tart and tangy salad will make it feel like a day at the beach. Be sure to clean the grapefruit and pomelo segments well to ensure that each bite is smooth.

16 jumbo shrimp, peeled and deveined
16 scallops
⅓ cup olive oil
1 large red grapefruit, peeled and divided into segments
1 pomelo, peeled and divided into segments
1 bunch arugula
1 teaspoon coarse salt
½ teaspoon ground black pepper
Freshly squeezed juice from ½ lemon

1. Preheat grill.
2. Brush shrimp and scallops with olive oil. Oil the grill grate. Place the shrimp and scallops on the grill grate and grill over a high flame, turning to sear on both sides, for about 2 minutes. Remove shrimp and scallops from grill.
3. In a bowl, combine the grilled seafood, grapefruit, pomelo and arugula. Season with salt, pepper and lemon juice.
4. Set aside for 5 minutes to allow the flavors to be absorbed. Transfer to dinner plates and serve.

SMOKED SALMON

Makes **10** to **15** servings

1 pound coarse salt
1 pound natural brown sugar
4 pounds salmon fillets, boneless and with skin
Fresh sprigs of rosemary and thyme, for firebox

🔥 **A note from the chef:** The woody sweetness of smoked salmon is always a crowd pleaser. Serve hot with a heaped side of Mashed Potatoes with Garlic Confit (page 64), or substitute smoked salmon for the chicken in The King's Chicken Caesar Salad (page 62).

1. In a bowl, mix the salt and sugar.
2. Sprinkle half of the mixture onto a baking tray large enough to hold all the salmon. Place the salmon on the tray and cover with the remaining mixture. Chill in a refrigerator overnight.
3. The following day, remove the salmon from the mixture, rinse it with water and dry thoroughly with a paper towel.
4. **Prepare the smoker:** Mix rosemary and thyme sprigs with moistened sawdust and woodchips in the firebox.
5. Smoke the salmon at a temperature of 200°F to 225°F for 30 to 40 minutes.
6. Using a thick barbecue mitt, remove the salmon from the smoker and transfer to a platter on the kitchen counter. Cover the platter with aluminum foil and let the salmon rest for 20 minutes. This will allow the juices to gel, improving its taste and texture.

Storage instructions: Smoked Salmon can be stored in the refrigerator in a plastic wrap poked with holes for up to 1 week, or in the freezer in a freezer storage container for up to 2 months.

HERB-SMOKED TROUT

Makes

10

servings

🔥 **A note from the chef:** Make extra servings of this delicious fish for a flavor booster in your salads, pastas and soups.

For the Brine:
12½ cups water
1½ cups sea salt
½ cup natural brown sugar

6 whole trout, about 1 pound each, gutted and cleaned
Fresh sprigs of rosemary and thyme, for firebox

1. **Prepare the Brine:** In a large bowl, mix the water, salt and sugar.
2. Soak the trout in the Brine in the refrigerator for at least 1 day and up to 3 days.
3. Once marinated, remove the fish from the Brine, rinse with water, and dry thoroughly.
4. **Prepare the smoker:** Mix rosemary and thyme sprigs with moistened sawdust and woodchips in the firebox.
5. Smoke the trout at a temperature of 200°F to 225°F for 30 to 40 minutes, or until it gains a golden-honey hue.
6. Using a thick barbecue mitt, remove the trout from the smoker and transfer to dinner plates. Serve immediately.

Storage instructions: Smoked Trout can be stored in the refrigerator in a plastic wrap poked with holes for up to 1 week, or in the freezer in a freezer storage container for up to 2 months.

SMOKED SALMON SALAD WITH CASHEWS & HERBS

Makes

6

servings

🔥 **A note from the chef:** This crispy salad is so addictive you can be certain there won't be any leftovers. Almonds and pecans are fine substitutes if you don't have any cashews in your pantry.

1 pound Smoked Salmon (page 128), filleted, crumbled
2 bunches parsley, finely chopped
1 bunch cilantro, finely chopped
½ cup olive oil
¼ cup freshly squeezed lemon juice
1 cup cashew nuts, finely chopped
Coarse salt, to taste
Ground black pepper, to taste

1. In a large bowl, combine the Smoked Salmon, parsley, cilantro, olive oil, lemon juice and cashew nuts.
2. Taste and adjust seasoning with salt and pepper, and serve.

Storage instructions: This fish dish can be stored in an airtight container in the refrigerator for up to 2 days.

POTATO SALAD WITH HERB-SMOKED TROUT FILLET

🔥 **A note from the chef:** This innovative potato recipe defies the old paradigm of mayonnaise-heavy potato salad and transforms it into a hearty summer salad that satisfies without weighing you down. Smoked salmon or anchovies can be used in place of trout.

For the Dressing:
1 teaspoon mustard
¼ cup olive oil
¼ cup white wine vinegar
Juice from ½ lemon
1 garlic clove, crushed
1 teaspoon sugar
Coarse salt, to taste
Ground black pepper, to taste

For the Salad:
2 pounds baby potatoes, cooked, peeled and halved
1 large purple onion, halved and julienned
3½ ounces Kalamata olives, about 25 olives, pitted
½ bunch dill, coarsely chopped
2 pounds Herb-Smoked Trout (page 129), filleted, crumbled

1. **Prepare the Dressing:** In a bowl, combine the mustard, olive oil, vinegar, lemon juice, garlic and sugar. Taste and adjust seasoning with salt and pepper.
2. **Prepare the Salad:** In a large bowl, combine the potatoes, onion, olives and dill. Add the Herb-Smoked Trout to the salad, drizzle with Dressing, and toss lightly. Let the salad sit for 1 hour before serving.

Storage instructions: This fish dish can be stored in an airtight container in the refrigerator for up to 2 days.

SMOKED SALMON & CREAM CHEESE BAGEL

Makes

4

servings

4 large bagels, split
1 cup cream cheese
1 pound Smoked Salmon, crumbled [page 128]

1. Place the bagels, cut-side down, on the grill to toast until light grill marks appear.
2. Using grilling tongs, remove bagels from grill. Transfer bagels to dinner plates. Spread cream cheese on both halves of each bagel.
3. Top with a generous portion of Smoked Salmon, and serve.

A note from the chef: Serving homemade smoked salmon atop a toasted bagel is a great way to add sophistication to a simple classic. For added crunch and texture, pile on fresh cucumber and purple onion.

05
SWEET
ENDINGS

CINNAMON PEAR KABOBS

Makes

4

servings

4 tablespoons butter
4 firm pears, cores removed
4 cinnamon sticks
2 teaspoons cinnamon
4 teaspoons brown sugar
4 tablespoons walnuts, crushed

For serving:
Vanilla ice cream (optional)

🔥 **A note from the chef:** These delightful grilled pears will satisfy your sweet tooth without an undue amount of sugar. If you're a fan of citrusy flavors, try soaking cored pears in orange juice for ½ an hour before cooking them.

1. Preheat grill.
2. Place a small amount of butter over the pear holes and use the cinnamon stick to push the butter into the pear cores. The cinnamon stick should be firmly planted inside the pear, about halfway through.
3. Insert the remaining butter into the top of the hole. Season with cinnamon, brown sugar and walnuts, and cover the pears with aluminum foil.
4. Place the pears on the preheated grill, cinnamon stick side up so that the cinnamon sticks don't burn.
5. Grill for 20 minutes. Using grilling tongs, remove pears from grill. Unwrap the aluminum foil, and serve hot. Cinnamon Pear Kabobs can be served with a scoop of vanilla ice cream.

GRILLED BANANAS WITH CHOCOLATE

Makes

4

servings

4 bananas
8-12 squares milk or bittersweet chocolate

1. Preheat grill.
2. Place the bananas in the peels on the grill grate. Grill on each side until the banana is entirely browned, for about 10 minutes.
3. Using a sharp knife, make a slit along most of the length of the unpeeled banana skin and almost through the bananas.
4. Push 2-3 cubes of chocolate into the slit of each banana. Let the heat from the banana melt the chocolate (it will take about 1 minute).
5. Serve in the peel with a spoon to scoop out the cooked banana flesh and melted chocolate.

GRILLED TROPICAL FRUIT SUNDAE

Makes

4

servings

4 tablespoons honey
1 tablespoon lemon juice
1 large pineapple, peeled and sliced
1 mango, peeled and quartered
Ice cream

1. Preheat grill.
2. Warm the honey and lemon juice in a small pot on the grill.
3. Brush the pineapple and mango with the honey-lemon sauce and grill until lightly singed on both sides, occasionally turning and brushing with additional sauce.
4. Using grilling tongs, transfer to a serving dish. Top the fruit with a scoop of ice cream, drizzle the remaining honey-lemon sauce over it, and serve.

A note from the chef: For best results, use ripe pineapple and select a mango that is not too soft. I recommend serving cinnamon ice cream or berry sorbet on top of the fruit.

MASCARPONE & GRILLED STRAWBERRY PANCAKES

Makes

4

servings

30 fresh strawberries
4 tablespoons sugar
Whiskey (for soaking strawberries)
Basic Pancakes [page 36]
½ cup mascarpone cheese

1. Preheat grill.
2. Place strawberries and sugar in a metal bowl. Cover with whiskey, transfer to the refrigerator, and let the strawberries marinate for 3 to 4 hours.
3. Remove the strawberries from the liquid and set the liquid aside. Sear the strawberries on the grill for about 2 minutes and transfer to a serving dish.
4. Place the metal bowl with the marinade on the grill and heat for 3 minutes.
5. Place the strawberries atop warm Basic Pancakes and add a dollop of mascarpone cheese. Drizzle with warm whiskey-sugar sauce and serve.

A note from the chef: This delectable dessert pancake can be enjoyed with almost any fruit. Try it with peaches, pineapple, or mango.